Preface

Professional skills and ethics are vital in shaping competent, ethical professionals equipped to navigate today's complex work environment. These subjects are integral to modern education, instilling in students the ability to act with integrity, responsibility, and sound judgment in their careers. Recognizing their importance, the Indira Gandhi National Open University (IGNOU) has made these topics a core part of its curriculum, pushing students to master both theoretical concepts and practical applications.

This book, IGNOU MCS-214 Professional Skills and Ethics Previous Years Unsolved Papers, is a carefully curated compilation of unsolved question papers from previous years. It serves as an essential resource for students preparing for exams, helping them assess their understanding, identify weaknesses, and improve their problem-solving skills.Practicing with past papers is a proven method for effective exam preparation. It not only familiarizes students with the types and formats of questions but also deepens their understanding by applying concepts to practical scenarios. By working through these unsolved papers, students can gauge their exam readiness, enhance time management, and build confidence in tackling challenging questions.

The decision to leave these papers unsolved encourages active engagement, critical thinking, and exploration of multiple problem-solving approaches. This method fosters independent learning, better preparing students for the variety of questions they may face in exams.Covering a broad spectrum of topics-communication skills, leadership, workplace ethics, and legal considerations—this book provides thorough coverage of the syllabus, ensuring students grasp the essential concepts for exam success.We hope this book supports your academic journey and inspires deeper exploration into professional skills and ethics. The knowledge gained here will undoubtedly be invaluable in shaping your future career. Wishing you success in your studies and future endeavors in the professional world.

Table of Contents

Chapter 1: Term-End Examination, December, 2021
MCS-214, Professional Skills and Ethics

Time : 2 Hours
Maximum Marks : 50
Note : Answer all questions.

1. Read the following passage and answer the questions below it :

Once you've mastered reading the cues and emotions of other people, you're ready to read an entire room. It may sound daunting, but it's what you've already learned about social awareness—just on a larger scale.

Essentially, there are two ways to pick up the mood of an entire room. First, you can rely solely on your gut instincts. Emotions are contagious, meaning they spread from one or two people until there's a palpable and collective mood that you will feel at some level.

For example, imagine walking into a room of 125 entrepreneurs who are networking and sharing their ideas. It's pretty likely that there would be excitement and positive energy there, and it wouldn't take long to become aware of it. You'd hear their voice levels and tones, and see the focused and interested posture and body language. Now imagine walking into a room of 125 people waiting to be chosen for jury duty

The room is quiet; people are trying to distract themselves with reading material, music, and anything else to pass the time. Even though it's our civic duty to attend, hardly anyone wants to be there. The two moods are like night and day.Here's how you can catch the mood of the room.When you enter the room, scan it and notice whether you feel and see energy or quiet, subdued calm. Take notice of how people are arranging themselves—alone or in groups. Are they talking and moving their hands ? Are some more animated than others ? What is your gut telling you about them ?

Another way to read the mood of the room is to bring along a more experienced guide, much like you would on an African safari. Your guide should be a socially aware expert willing to show you the ropes when it comes to tapping into your instincts and picking up the room's mood. Shadow your guide and listen to what he feels and sees. Ask what he senses and what clues gave the mood away. Eventually, you should be in one to take the lead.

Questions :

(a) Answer the following questions :

(i) What do you think the author means by 'the mood of the room' ? 2

(ii) Discuss the two ways to "pick up the mood of the room." Give examples. 2+2

(iii) What does the author suggest that we should do to 'catch' the mood of the room ? 2

(iv) Give a title to the passage and give reasons for it. 2

(b) Find words/phrases from the passage which mean the same as the following : 6

(i) signs/prompts (para 1)

(ii) intimidating/frightening (para 1)

(iii) transmittable (para 2)

(iv) business person (para 2)

(v) instinctive feeling (para 3)

(vi) evaluate the room (para 4)

(c) Make sentences of your own with the following words/phrases from the passage : 4

(i) Emotions

(ii) Networking

(iii) Distract

(iv) hone your ability

2. Write short notes on any two of the following : 5 each

(i) The qualities of a star performer

(ii) Building self-confidence

(iii) What constitutes plagiarism ?

(iv) Leading an ethical life both personally and

(v) professionally.

3. (i) Fill in the blanks with a/an, the or no article : 0.5 each

The larger _________ meeting, the more difficult it becomes to reach at __________ decision. __________ ideal size of __________ meeting depends on _________ purpose of ___________ meeting. If __________ meeting has been called to take __________ decision on any matter, it is advisable to call just __________ few individuals for it. All ___________ meetings have something in common.

(ii) Rewrite the sentences below beginning with the words given below : 5

(a) The crop has been destroyed due to heavy rainfall.
Heavy rainfall ______________________

(b) We will hold the meeting on the 10th of this month.
The meeting _______________________

(c) The house is being sold.
They ___________________________

(d) You are requested to maintain silence.
Please ________________________

(e) The college has organised an inter- college debate competition.
An inter-college _____________________

4. Write a letter to a friend about your new job in an IT company. Talk about : 10

(i) The work you do
(ii) The satisfaction you derive from it □
(iii) Your supportive and friendly colleagues

You may use about **150** words.

Chapter 2: Term-End Examination, June, 2022
MCS-214, Professional Skills and Ethics

Time : 2 Hours
Maximum Marks : 50
Note : Answer all questions.

1. Read the following passage and answer the questions below it : 20

Competition is a fact of life. To pretend that it doesn't exist or that you should avoid it all costs would be ridiculous. I've always loved to compete. As a child I was the fastest runner at school and the number one tennis player in Northern California in my age group. I was a high school All-American Athlete and went on to receive a college scholarship in tennis, where I played in the number one position and became the youngest captain in my team's history. I've run three marathons, one of them in three hours.

As an adult, my love of competition has continued, not only in sports, but in business as well. I love to negotiate, buy low, and sell high. I'm proud to be creative, and I'd like to believe I have a flair for marketing. The publishing world is fiercely competitive. I love to see my books doing well, and it's fun to get a standing ovation after a speech. I could certainly make the argument that if I didn't compete well, I wouldn't be helping very many people. So it's important that I compete. I tell you these things because I've spoken to many people who assume that I'm too relaxed to compete, which is not true. I don't want to give the impression, as I suggest you compete from the heart, that you can't compete effectively if you are a gentle person and become less attached to winning. You can have it all. You can be a winner and financially successful, have fun, compete hard, but never lose your perspective of what's most important—enjoying yourself, giving back, and taking it all in stride.

To compete from the heart means that you compete less from a desperate or neurotic need to achieve and more out of a love for what you do. Competing is its own reward. You are completely immersed in the process, absorbed
in the present moments of the activity— the business deal, the sale, the negotiation, interaction, or whatever. When you compete from your heart, the process itself provides the satisfaction; winning is secondary. When looked at in this healthier way, your business life becomes so much easier. You play hard—and then let go. You bounce back almost instantly.

You're resilient. You're a good sport. By not being so attached to a specific outcome (winning), you conserve energy and see hidden opportunities. You learn from your mistakes and losses. You move forward. Isn't it obvious that this not-so-attached attitude is in your best interest ? It's been said, "Winning isn't everything, it's the only thing." To me, this is utter nonsense.

This philosophy stems from the fear that if you aren't consumed with winning, you never will win. I can tell you that I'm not consumed with winning—never have been, never will be—yet I've won many awards, contests, and first-place finishes. I've also done well financially and made some wise investments. But none of my competitive accomplishments would mean anything to me if they weren't from the heart—
if I became so carried away with the competition and outcome that I forgot my humanity. So, to me, the "Winning is everything" motto is grossly inaccurate.

(a) (i) What were the two things that the author excelled in, in his childhood ? How did this benefit him ? 2

(ii) What do you think is the author's profession(s) ? Why ? 2

(iii) Describe the "new" way of competing that the author suggests in para 3. 2

(iv) The author believes in "complete from the heart." What do you think this means ? How is this philosophy different from "winning is everything" ? Discus. 4

(b) Find words/phrases from the passage which mean the same as the following : 5

(i) talent (para 2)
(ii) great applause (para 2)
(iii) to deal with a difficult situation in a calm way (para 3)
(iv) quick to recover (para 4)
(v) totally preoccupied (para 5)

(c) Make sentences with the following words/ phrases : 5

(i) Marathons
(ii) Perspective
(iii) Neurotic
(iv) bounce back
(v) accomplishments

2. Write short notes on any two of the following : 2×5=10

(i) A brief history of copyright law
(ii) Ethics at the workplace
(iii) Personal and social competence
(iv) What are "blindspots" and how to overcome them ?
(v) Collaboration and cooperation
(vi) Presentation skills

3. (a) Fill in the blanks using the linking words given below : 5

There is one extra linker given :

yet, although, in spite of, unless, because, moreover

(i) You can't take the exam _______________ you have 75% attendance.

(ii) The building looks old _______________ it being maintained regularly.

(iii) She couldn't reach on time _______________ the bus broke down on the way.

(iv) She is not very resourceful _______________ she is always ready to help everyone.

(v) _______________ he is quite old, he works very fast.

(b) Look at the following answers and form suitable questions : 5

(i) Yes, I'll go with you.

(ii) I met her at a party.

(iii) Of course, I can visit you tomorrow.

(iv) I suggest you exercise for 45 minutes every day.

(v) No, it is not possible.

4. You ordered for an i-pad on an online retailing service and you received a defective piece. Draft a letter to the head of Consumer Grievances of that organization indicating this and request for the replacement of the product. 10

Chapter 3: Term-End Examination, December, 2022
MCS-214, Professional Skills and Ethics

Time : 2 Hours
Maximum Marks : 50
Note : Answer all questions.

1. Read the following passage and answer the questions below it :

The world is often a dangerous place to do business in. For an organization to survive it must become adept at identifying and managing possible risks. In our personal lives we do this every day, often without thinking about it. Before we cross the road, we look around to make sure there isn't a vehicle heading towards us. And every parent weighs up all potential dangers before allowing their child to run the risk of riding a bike outside.
Businesses have to make predicting, recognizing, and minimizing risk as natural and habitual as this. Some risks affect all businesses, such as the unpredictability of economics (e.g. inflation), politics (e.g. new legislation), and business realities (e.g. late payments). However, there are also risks specific to each sector. In the volatile telecommunications sector, a mobile phone company has to anticipate shifting customer taste in a market that is moving so fast it's hard to look one year into the future, let alone ten.
It's been said that the species most likely to survive is the one most responsive to change. The problem in risk assessment is that progression and change in today's world is no longer linear and predictable. The only successful business will be one that accepts uncertainty and is flexible enough to respond to change as it comes. That's where Watchman can help. This impressive software accepts a variety of inputs and then produces a stunning three-dimensional graphic display that allows you to view various risk factors at a glance,all against an interactive timeline. Intuitive controls allow you to filter the output to compare probabilities, determine the relative importance of each risk factor, and evaluate potential impact. And, of course, you can alter the variables to gauge how different conditions make an impact — in the hope that this knowledge will help you to avoid exposing your organization to unnecessary risks.
So it's great as far as it goes, but there is a problem. If the input you provide is incomplete, this will affect the quality of the risk analysis. Watchman can't do the thinking for you and it can't determine whether a threat is directly relevant to your company. It is a sound program, but it is no replacement for the skilled, intuitive work done by an experienced risk manager.

(a) Answer the following questions based on the passage :

i. What are the risks that all businesses face at some time or the other ? 2

ii. What makes a business successful according to the passage ? 2

iii. What is 'Watchman' according to the passage ? How does it help a business reduce its risk factors ? 2

iv. When does 'Watchman' not perform to its optimum ? Why ? 2

v. Give an appropriate title to the passage and explain why it is appropriate. 2

(b) Find words from the passage which mean the same as the following phrases/words : 5

i. proficient/good at (para 1)

ii. forecasting (para 1)

iii. changeable/ever-changing (para 2)

iv. instinctive (para 3)

v. to check out (para 3)

(c) Make sentences with the following words/phrases : 5

i. survive
ii. minimizing
iii. anticipate
iv. stunning
v. evaluate

2. Write short notes on any two of the following : 10

(a) Barriers to communication

(b) Characteristics and conventions of conversation

(c) How to be successful in a group discussion

(d) Qualities that employees must develop if they want to be successful

(e) A brief history of Copyright

3. (a) Write down the questions that led to each of these answers. The first one is done for you as an example. 5

i. Q : Are you Ms. Sen ?
A : That's right. Pleased to meet you.

ii. Q : ______ ?
A : Yes thanks. I had a very good flight.

iii. Q : ______ ?
A : I would like to meet Mr. Prakash, if he's in the office.

iv. Q : ______ ?
A : No, my husband is travelling with me. I'm meeting him later.

v. Q : ______ ?
A : It was Mr. Jain who recommended the hotel to me.

(b) Fill in the blanks with a/an, the or no article. 5

More and more ____________ shoppers are by-passing _____________ brand names for ___________ cheaper no-name products. This shows that even ___________ biggest and strongest brands in __________ world are vulnerable.

4. Write a brief article in about 250 words on any one of the following topics : 10

a) Technology in the Classroom is the New Normal
b) The World as a Global Village
c) Protection of the Environment for the sake of the Future Generations
d) The Impact of the Internet on Social Relations
e) AI in the Household.

Chapter 4: Term-End Examination, June, 2023
MCS-214, Professional Skills and Ethics

Time : 2 Hours
Maximum Marks : 50
Note : Answer all questions.

1. Read the following passage and answer the questions below it :

One of the greatest advances of modern technology has been the invention of computers. They are widely used in industries and universities. Now there is hardly any sphere of human life where computers have not been pressed into service of humans. We are heading fast towards a day when a computer will be as much a part of our daily life as a telephone or a computer. Computers are capable of doing extremely complicated work in all branches of learning. They can solve the most complex mathematical problems or put thousands of unrelated facts into order. These machines can be put to various uses. For instance, they can provide information in the best way to prevent traffic jams.

The process by which machines can be used to work for us has been called 'automation'. In the future, automation may enable human beings to enjoy more leisure than they do today. The coming of automation is bound to have important social consequences.Some years ago, an expert on automation, Sir Leon Bagrit pointed out that it was a mistake to believe that these machines could 'think'.There is no possibility that human beings will be 'controlled by machines'.

Though computers are capable of learning from their mistakes and improving their performance, they need detailed instructions from human beings to operate. They can never, as it were, lead independent lives or 'rule the world' by making decisions on their own. Sir Leon said that in future, computers would be developed which would be small enough to carry in a pocket. Ordinary people would then be able to use them to obtain valuable information.

Computers could be plugged into a national network and be used like radios. For instance, people going on holiday could be informed about the weather conditions. Car drivers can be given alternative routes when there are traffic jams. It will also be possible to make tiny translating machines. This will enable people who do not share a common language to talk to each other without any difficulty.

Question :

(a) Answer the following questions : 5×2=10

i. Explain automation.

ii. Why can't computers lead independent lives or rule the world ? Give two reasons.

iii. What are Sir Leon's views on automation ?

iv. Give the meaning of the following phrases :
(i) 'Controlled by machine'
(ii) 'Rule the world'

v. Give a suitable title to the passage and give reason for it.

(b) Find words or phrases from the passage that mean the some as following : 6

i. Make progress (Para 1)

ii. Creation (Pare 1)

iii. Precious (Pare 2)

iv. Having the ability (Para 2)

v. Available as another possibility (Para 3)

vi. A way or course (Para 3)

(c) Make sentences of your own with the following words/phrases from the passage : 4

i. Widely

ii. Complicated

iii. Possibility

iv. Conditions

2. Write short notes on any two of the following in about 75 words each : 5×2=10

i. The qualities of a leader

ii. Problem solving skills

iii. Importance of feedback in communication

iv. Why is honesty the best policy ?

3. (I) Fill in the blanks with a, an, the or no article : 5

I am from Mumbai, Maharashtra. Mumbai is ___________ city in ___________ India. I live in ___________ house in ___________ quiet street in ___________ countryside ___________ street is called 'Malad street' and ___________ house is more than 100 years old. I work as _____________ librarian at ____________ college near ___________ town.

II. Rewrite the sentences beginning with the words given below : 5

i. The train has been delayed due to heavy floods.

Heavy floods ____________________________

ii. We will buy a car by next year.
A car _________________________________

iii. The game is played by them.
They __________________________________

iv. The parents requested the children to participate in Olympiad.
Please _________________________________

v. The University has launched a vocational course.
A vocational course ______________________

4. Write a letter to your parents informing them about your internship at a Tech-firm HCL. Talk about : 10

i. Your work profile

ii. The incentives provided by workplace

iii. The challenges that you faced and overcome

You may use about **150** words.

Chapter 5: Term-End Examination, December, 2023
MCS-214, Professional Skills and Ethics

Time : 2 Hours
Maximum Marks : 50
Note : Answer all questions.

1. Read the following passage and answer the questions below it :Information Technology (IT) is the application of computers and internet to store, retrieve, transmit and manipulate information, often in the context of a business or other enterprise. IT is considered as a subset of Information and Communication Technology (ICT) and has evolved according to the needs. It is worth noting that the term IT is commonly used as a synonym for computers and it has, in this sense, shaped societies and adapted itself to people's needs. Humans were the first 'computers'. Then machines were invented to carry out computational tasks. Now these machines have given way to a new form of information technology. Information has become accessible from anywhere through cloud technology. The term information technology in its modern sense first appeared in a 1958 article published in the Harvard Business Review; authors Harold J. Leavitt and Thomas I. Whisler commented that the new technology does not yet have a single established name. We shall call it Information Technology (IT). Their definition consists of three categories: techniques for processing, the application of statistical and mathematical methods to decision-making and the simulation of higher-order thinking through computer programs and computer networks but it also encompasses other information distribution technologies such as television and telephones. Several industries are associated with information technology including computer hardware, software, electronics, semiconductors, internet, telecom equipment, engineering, health care, e-commerce, and computer services.

Thanks to the continuous development of computers, the original computing systems became minicomputers and later personal computers took the lead. Nowadays, mobile phones are dethroning the personal computer and computing is evolving faster to become disembodied like a cloud, becoming accessible more easily whenever needed. Information technology has transformed people and companies and has allowed digital technology to influence society and the economy alike.

Questions:

(a) Answer the following questions: $5 \times 2 = 10$

i. Information technology is evolving mostly as a result of?
ii. The author claims that the first computers were?
iii. What is the outcome of the development of information technology?
iv. What does it signify when computing systems take the shape of clouds?
v. Give a suitable title to the passage and give a reason for it.

(b) Find words or phrases from the passage that mean the same as the following: 6

i. A place where items may be kept (Para 1)

ii. To spend or convey from one person or place to another (Para 1)
iii. Modify (Para 1)
iv. To create (Para 2)
v. A result or effect of an action or condition (Para 2)
vi. Imitate (Para 2)

(c) Make sentences of your own with the following words from the passage: 4

i. Retrieve
ii. Subset
iii. Dethrone
iv. Accessible

2. Write short notes on any two of the following: 5×2=10

(i) Should anonymity be allowed on the internet?
(ii) How important is time management?
(iii) Your understanding of morality and ethics
(iv) Impact of social media.

3. (a) Fill in the blanks with a, an, the, or no article: 10×1/2=5

To say education is important is _____________ understatement. It is ______________ weapon to improve one's life. It is probably ______ most important to bring about social change. Education for _______________ child begins at home. It is ______ lifelong process that ends with death. Education certainly determines ______________ quality of ______________ individual's life. Education improves one's knowledge skill and develops _____________ personality and attitude most noteworthy. Education affects _______________ chance of employment for people. A highly educated individual is probably very likely to get _____________ good job.

(b) Rewrite the following sentences beginning with the word given below: 5

i. The girl has been feeling sick because of the weather.
Bad weather …

ii. I will write a book in the next semester.
A book …

iii. Your food is being prepared by him.
He is …

iv. You are requested to throw garbage in the dustbin.
Please …

v. She has stitched a new uniform for her sister.
A new uniform ...

4. Write a letter to your friend sharing details of a newly offered course in your university. 10
Talk about:

(i) How innovative and different this course
(ii) Your ideas and understanding about the course
(iii) The scope of the course

You may use about 150 words.

Chapter 6: Most Asked Questions Part-A

1. What are professional ethics, and why are they important in the IT industry?
Answer: Professional ethics refer to the set of moral principles and standards that govern the behavior of professionals in their workplace. In the IT industry, ethics are critical because professionals often handle sensitive data, intellectual property, and systems that impact society. Ethical conduct ensures trustworthiness, prevents misuse of technology, and supports compliance with laws and regulations. For instance, respecting user privacy, avoiding software piracy, and adhering to cybersecurity practices are essential. Professional ethics also build credibility for IT professionals and organizations, fostering long-term success and societal well-being.

2. Define professional skills and their relevance for MCA graduates.
Answer: Professional skills are the soft and technical abilities that enable individuals to perform effectively in their work environment. For MCA graduates, these skills include communication, teamwork, time management, problem-solving, and technical proficiency in programming and system design. Strong professional skills are vital in collaborating with diverse teams, handling client requirements, and adapting to fast-changing technologies. These skills enhance employability, ensure smooth project execution, and contribute to career growth by making graduates versatile and capable in dynamic IT environments.

3. Discuss the key principles of professional conduct in software development.
Answer: Key principles of professional conduct in software development include integrity, accountability, confidentiality, fairness, and respect. Integrity ensures honesty in coding and reporting progress. Accountability involves taking responsibility for one's work and decisions. Confidentiality safeguards client and user data, preventing unauthorized access. Fairness means avoiding discrimination and treating all stakeholders equally. Respect fosters healthy team dynamics and collaboration. Adhering to these principles helps software developers maintain ethical standards, deliver high-quality products, and uphold public trust in technology.

4. What is the significance of a code of ethics for IT professionals?
Answer: A code of ethics provides IT professionals with guidelines for ethical decision-making and behavior in their work. It outlines acceptable practices, promotes integrity, and helps resolve ethical dilemmas. For instance, professional bodies like ACM and IEEE have codes that emphasize protecting user privacy, avoiding conflicts of interest, and ensuring software quality. Such codes enhance professional credibility, encourage self-regulation, and ensure that IT practices align with societal and legal expectations, fostering a responsible and sustainable technology ecosystem.

5. Explain the role of teamwork in professional success.
Answer: Teamwork is crucial for professional success as it enables individuals to collaborate effectively toward common goals. In the IT sector, complex projects often require contributions from developers, designers, testers, and managers. Good teamwork promotes knowledge sharing, creativity, and faster problem-solving. It also helps in distributing workload efficiently and improving morale. For MCA graduates, mastering teamwork skills ensures seamless integration into organizations and enhances their ability to thrive in multidisciplinary environments where collaboration is key to project success.

6. How does communication skill impact professional growth?
Answer: Communication skills impact professional growth by enabling clear expression of ideas, fostering collaboration, and building strong relationships with colleagues and clients. In IT, professionals often need to explain technical concepts to non-technical stakeholders, making effective communication critical. Strong skills in verbal, written, and digital communication help avoid misunderstandings, improve project outcomes, and position individuals as leaders. For MCA graduates, these skills enhance job performance, open opportunities for leadership roles, and contribute to long-term career advancement.

7. Discuss the importance of time management for IT professionals.
Answer: Time management is vital for IT professionals due to the demanding nature of software development and project deadlines. Effective time management ensures tasks are prioritized, resources are utilized efficiently, and project milestones are met. Poor time management can lead to stress, errors, and missed deadlines, affecting team

performance and client satisfaction. MCA graduates who develop this skill can balance multiple responsibilities, adapt to tight schedules, and increase productivity, making them valuable assets in any organization.

8. What is meant by professional responsibility in the workplace?
Answer: Professional responsibility in the workplace refers to an individual's commitment to fulfilling their duties ethically, competently, and reliably. It involves adhering to organizational policies, delivering quality work, respecting colleagues, and upholding confidentiality. In IT, professionals are responsible for ensuring system security, protecting user data, and avoiding practices like plagiarism or software piracy. By embracing professional responsibility, MCA graduates can build trust with employers and clients, contribute positively to organizational goals, and maintain their reputation in the industry.

9. Explain the concept of work ethics and its impact on organizational culture.
Answer: Work ethics encompass a set of values such as honesty, diligence, punctuality, and commitment that guide behavior in the workplace. Strong work ethics positively influence organizational culture by fostering accountability, trust, and productivity. Employees with good work ethics set high standards, inspire peers, and contribute to a collaborative and respectful environment. For IT companies, a culture grounded in strong work ethics enhances innovation, reduces conflicts, and attracts top talent, leading to long-term organizational success.

10. Discuss the ethical issues related to privacy in the digital era.
Answer: Privacy in the digital era involves protecting personal information from unauthorized access, misuse, and exposure. Ethical issues arise when organizations collect, store, or share user data without consent. Examples include data breaches, surveillance without transparency, and selling user information to third parties. IT professionals must address these concerns by implementing robust security measures, adhering to privacy laws like GDPR, and respecting user rights. Ethical handling of privacy issues is essential to maintain user trust and prevent legal consequences.

11. What are intellectual property rights, and why are they important in IT?
Answer: Intellectual property rights (IPR) protect creations of the mind, such as software, designs, and inventions, from unauthorized use or duplication. In IT, IPR ensures that developers, organizations, and innovators receive recognition and financial rewards for their work. It covers copyrights, patents, trademarks, and trade secrets. Respecting IPR prevents plagiarism and promotes innovation by encouraging investment in research and development. For MCA graduates, understanding IPR is crucial to avoid legal violations and contribute ethically to the IT industry.

12. Explain how ethical decision-making affects professional reputation.
Answer: Ethical decision-making involves choosing actions that align with moral principles and professional standards. It directly impacts an individual's reputation by reflecting their integrity and reliability. For instance, an IT professional who refuses to participate in unethical practices like hacking or software piracy earns respect from colleagues and clients. Conversely, unethical decisions can damage trust, harm careers, and lead to legal repercussions. MCA graduates with strong ethical foundations build long-term credibility, enhancing their professional opportunities and standing in the industry.

13. Discuss the importance of adaptability as a professional skill in IT.
Answer: Adaptability is the ability to adjust to new technologies, workflows, and work environments. In IT, rapid advancements mean professionals must continually learn and evolve. Adaptable employees embrace change, solve problems creatively, and thrive under pressure. For MCA graduates, adaptability enhances employability and career resilience, as it enables them to transition smoothly between roles, industries, or technologies. Organizations value adaptable professionals for their flexibility and willingness to contribute effectively in dynamic environments.

14. How can IT professionals contribute to corporate social responsibility (CSR)?
Answer: IT professionals contribute to CSR by developing sustainable technologies, promoting digital literacy, and ensuring ethical practices in their organizations. They can design energy-efficient systems, participate in community outreach programs, and support initiatives like open-source projects for public good. Data privacy, cybersecurity awareness, and inclusive software design are other areas where IT experts make a difference. For MCA graduates, actively engaging in CSR enhances their professional value and demonstrates their commitment to societal and environmental well-being.

15. Explain the concept of conflict resolution and its importance in professional settings.
Answer: Conflict resolution involves addressing disagreements constructively to reach a mutually beneficial outcome. In professional settings, unresolved conflicts can harm team morale and productivity. Effective conflict resolution requires empathy, communication, and problem-solving skills. IT professionals often work in collaborative environments where diverse opinions can lead to disputes. MCA graduates who master conflict resolution foster positive relationships, ensure smoother workflows, and contribute to a harmonious organizational culture, making them valuable team players and leaders.

16. What is professional integrity, and how does it impact the IT profession?
Answer: Professional integrity refers to adhering to moral and ethical principles such as honesty, fairness, and transparency in all professional activities. In the IT profession, integrity ensures that professionals do not engage in practices like data theft, plagiarism, or misrepresentation of information. It builds trust between employees, employers, and clients, leading to stronger relationships and better opportunities. For MCA graduates, demonstrating professional integrity fosters a positive reputation, encourages ethical leadership, and contributes to the credibility of the entire IT industry.

17. Discuss the role of critical thinking as a professional skill for MCA graduates.
Answer: Critical thinking enables professionals to analyze situations objectively, evaluate solutions, and make informed decisions. For MCA graduates, it is especially valuable in debugging complex code, designing system architectures, and resolving technical challenges. Critical thinking also helps in identifying risks and assessing the ethical implications of decisions in IT projects. This skill promotes innovation and ensures that professionals approach problems logically, reducing errors and improving overall efficiency in the workplace.

18. How do ethical issues arise in the use of artificial intelligence (AI)?
Answer: Ethical issues in AI arise due to biases in algorithms, privacy concerns, lack of transparency, and potential misuse. For example, AI systems may unintentionally discriminate against certain groups if trained on biased data. Autonomous systems like self-driving cars pose questions about accountability in case of accidents. MCA graduates working with AI must consider fairness, explainability, and compliance with legal standards to ensure responsible development and deployment of AI solutions that benefit society without causing harm.

19. Explain the concept of accountability in professional ethics.
Answer: Accountability in professional ethics refers to being answerable for one's actions, decisions, and their consequences in the workplace. It involves owning up to mistakes, learning from them, and ensuring corrective measures are taken. In IT, accountability is critical as professionals deal with sensitive data, critical systems, and user trust. MCA graduates who embrace accountability demonstrate reliability and professionalism, which strengthens team dynamics, minimizes risks, and promotes ethical organizational practices.

20. What are the ethical challenges in software piracy, and how can they be addressed?
Answer: Software piracy involves unauthorized copying, distribution, or use of software, violating intellectual property rights. Ethical challenges include revenue loss for creators, lack of motivation for innovation, and legal risks for users and organizations. Addressing piracy requires educating users about legal alternatives, enforcing copyright laws, and promoting open-source software where appropriate. MCA graduates should advocate for ethical use of software and adhere to licensing agreements, contributing to a fair and sustainable IT ecosystem.

21. Discuss how empathy enhances professional relationships in the workplace.
Answer: Empathy is the ability to understand and share the feelings of others, fostering stronger professional relationships. In the workplace, empathetic professionals listen actively, support colleagues during challenges, and resolve conflicts amicably. For MCA graduates entering team-based environments, empathy promotes collaboration, inclusivity, and trust, creating a positive organizational culture. It also helps in understanding client needs more effectively, leading to better solutions and higher customer satisfaction.

22. Explain the significance of lifelong learning in maintaining professional relevance.
Answer: Lifelong learning refers to continuously acquiring new knowledge and skills throughout one's career to remain relevant in a rapidly evolving industry. In IT, technologies change frequently, making lifelong learning

essential for MCA graduates. By staying updated with trends like cloud computing, cybersecurity, and AI, professionals enhance their adaptability and employability. Lifelong learners contribute more effectively to their organizations, innovate confidently, and enjoy sustained career growth in competitive job markets.

23. What is whistleblowing, and what ethical considerations are involved?
Answer: Whistleblowing occurs when an employee exposes unethical, illegal, or harmful practices within an organization. Ethical considerations include balancing loyalty to the organization with the responsibility to protect public interest. For instance, reporting data breaches or discriminatory practices can prevent significant harm but may risk retaliation. MCA graduates should be aware of whistleblower protections under law and carefully evaluate situations where whistleblowing aligns with professional ethics and societal responsibility.

24. Discuss the importance of cultural sensitivity as a professional skill in global IT environments.
Answer: Cultural sensitivity involves respecting and adapting to the diverse cultural backgrounds of colleagues and clients in global workplaces. For MCA graduates, this skill is crucial in IT environments where teams and customers may span multiple countries. Cultural sensitivity fosters better communication, minimizes misunderstandings, and promotes inclusivity. It enables professionals to navigate cross-cultural collaborations effectively, enhancing project outcomes and strengthening international business relationships.

25. Explain how ethical leadership influences organizational success.
Answer: Ethical leadership involves guiding teams with integrity, fairness, and a commitment to ethical standards. Such leaders set examples for others by prioritizing transparency, accountability, and respect in decision-making. In IT organizations, ethical leaders ensure responsible handling of data, fair treatment of employees, and compliance with legal norms. MCA graduates aspiring for leadership roles must embody ethical values to inspire trust, drive innovation, and contribute to sustainable organizational success.

26. What is the role of ethical hacking in promoting cybersecurity?
Answer: Ethical hacking involves authorized attempts to identify and fix vulnerabilities in computer systems and networks. Ethical hackers, often called penetration testers, simulate attacks to expose security flaws before malicious hackers can exploit them. This proactive approach strengthens cybersecurity by improving system defenses and protecting sensitive data. MCA graduates specializing in cybersecurity must adhere to strict ethical guidelines to ensure their actions benefit organizations and society. Ethical hacking supports compliance with regulations like GDPR and fosters user trust in digital platforms.

27. Discuss the importance of decision-making skills for IT professionals.
Answer: Decision-making skills enable IT professionals to analyze situations, evaluate options, and choose appropriate actions in complex and dynamic environments. In software development, decisions about design patterns, resource allocation, or troubleshooting directly impact project success. MCA graduates equipped with strong decision-making skills can navigate challenges confidently, balance technical and business requirements, and contribute to efficient workflows. Effective decision-making promotes innovation, minimizes risks, and ensures alignment with organizational goals.

28. Explain the concept of ethical dilemmas and provide an example in the IT context.
Answer: Ethical dilemmas occur when professionals face conflicting moral principles and must choose between two or more equally important values. In IT, an example is discovering a security flaw that could harm users if unreported but may also damage the company's reputation if disclosed. Resolving such dilemmas requires critical thinking, adherence to professional codes of ethics, and often consulting stakeholders. MCA graduates must develop ethical reasoning to handle such situations responsibly and align their decisions with both organizational and societal interests.

29. How do professional certifications enhance career prospects in IT?
Answer: Professional certifications validate an individual's expertise in specific technologies, tools, or methodologies, enhancing credibility in the job market. Certifications like AWS, PMP, or CISSP demonstrate commitment to learning and mastery of industry standards. For MCA graduates, earning certifications opens opportunities in specialized roles, increases salary prospects, and provides a competitive edge. Employers value certified professionals for their proven skills and readiness to handle critical IT tasks, contributing to organizational efficiency and success.

30. Discuss the role of problem-solving skills in software development.
Answer: Problem-solving skills are essential in software development for diagnosing bugs, optimizing algorithms, and designing efficient systems. IT professionals encounter challenges like integrating new technologies, meeting client requirements, or resolving system failures. Strong problem-solving abilities enable them to approach issues methodically, analyze root causes, and implement effective solutions. For MCA graduates, this skill ensures adaptability in fast-paced environments and positions them as reliable contributors to successful projects and innovations.

31. What are the ethical concerns surrounding artificial intelligence and automation?
Answer: Ethical concerns in AI and automation include job displacement, biased algorithms, privacy violations, and lack of accountability in autonomous systems. For example, AI-driven hiring tools may unintentionally discriminate if trained on biased datasets. MCA graduates working in AI must prioritize fairness, transparency, and adherence to ethical frameworks to mitigate risks. Developing explainable AI models and implementing robust data privacy measures ensures responsible innovation and protects public trust in automated systems.

32. Explain the importance of emotional intelligence in professional environments.
Answer: Emotional intelligence (EI) is the ability to recognize, understand, and manage one's emotions and those of others. In professional environments, EI fosters teamwork, leadership, and conflict resolution. IT professionals with high EI communicate effectively, adapt to stress, and build strong interpersonal relationships. For MCA graduates, developing EI is crucial for navigating diverse workplace dynamics, motivating colleagues, and ensuring collaboration in high-pressure projects, contributing to overall organizational success.

33. How can IT professionals address ethical challenges in data collection?
Answer: Ethical challenges in data collection include informed consent, data minimization, and protecting user privacy. IT professionals must ensure that data is collected transparently and used only for legitimate purposes. Techniques like anonymization and encryption safeguard sensitive information. Adherence to regulations such as GDPR or HIPAA is vital. MCA graduates should advocate ethical data practices, ensuring that organizations balance business needs with user rights, fostering trust and compliance in a data-driven world.

34. Discuss the role of negotiation skills in IT project management.
Answer: Negotiation skills are critical in IT project management for resolving conflicts, aligning stakeholder expectations, and managing resources effectively. Project managers often negotiate timelines, budgets, and deliverables with clients and team members. Strong negotiation fosters collaboration, prevents disputes, and ensures mutually beneficial outcomes. For MCA graduates aspiring to leadership roles, mastering negotiation enhances their ability to manage complex projects successfully and maintain healthy professional relationships.

35. What is the significance of professional networking for career advancement?
Answer: Professional networking involves building and maintaining relationships with peers, mentors, and industry leaders to exchange knowledge and explore opportunities. In IT, networking opens doors to collaborations, job referrals, and insights into emerging trends. For MCA graduates, attending conferences, participating in online forums, and joining professional associations expand their visibility and career prospects. Effective networking accelerates personal growth, keeps professionals informed, and creates pathways for mentorship and advancement in competitive environments.

36. Explain how ethical behavior affects client relationships in the IT industry.
Answer: Ethical behavior builds trust and credibility in client relationships by ensuring transparency, fairness, and accountability. IT professionals handling client data or delivering software solutions must avoid misrepresentation, protect confidentiality, and meet commitments diligently. For MCA graduates entering the workforce, demonstrating ethical conduct ensures long-term partnerships, enhances client satisfaction, and strengthens the organization's reputation in a competitive market. Ethical behavior is the foundation of sustainable business relationships.

37. Discuss the impact of digital addiction and the ethical responsibilities of IT professionals.
Answer: Digital addiction refers to excessive use of technology that negatively impacts mental and physical health. IT professionals developing apps or platforms have an ethical responsibility to design features that encourage healthy

usage patterns, such as time reminders and parental controls. MCA graduates working in technology must balance engagement strategies with user well-being, ensuring their innovations promote positive societal impact rather than exploiting addictive behaviors for profit.

38. What is plagiarism in the IT context, and how can it be avoided?
Answer: Plagiarism in IT involves using someone else's code, designs, or content without proper attribution. It is unethical and may result in legal consequences, loss of credibility, or academic penalties. MCA graduates can avoid plagiarism by writing original code, citing external sources, and using open-source licenses appropriately. Developing a habit of ethical coding and respecting intellectual property rights ensures professional integrity and fosters innovation in the IT industry.

39. Explain how professional ethics influence innovation in technology.
Answer: Professional ethics influence innovation by ensuring that new technologies are developed responsibly, with consideration for societal impact and user rights. Ethical innovators prioritize sustainability, accessibility, and fairness in their designs. For example, developing inclusive software that accommodates users with disabilities reflects ethical innovation. MCA graduates adhering to ethical standards contribute to technologies that solve real-world problems while upholding public trust and minimizing unintended negative consequences.

40. Discuss the role of stress management in maintaining professional productivity.
Answer: Stress management is crucial for maintaining focus, creativity, and efficiency in high-pressure IT environments. Chronic stress can lead to burnout, errors, and reduced job satisfaction. Techniques like time management, mindfulness, and regular breaks help professionals stay balanced and productive. For MCA graduates transitioning to demanding roles, mastering stress management ensures resilience, enhances performance, and supports long-term career success in the fast-paced technology sector.

41. What are the ethical considerations in open-source software development?
Answer: Ethical considerations in open-source development include respecting licenses, crediting contributors, and avoiding misuse of shared resources. Developers must ensure their contributions are transparent, secure, and do not violate intellectual property rights. For MCA graduates, participating ethically in open-source projects builds credibility and strengthens collaborative skills. Upholding ethical standards in open-source fosters a culture of trust, innovation, and mutual respect in the developer community.

42. Explain the significance of mentorship for professional development in IT.
Answer: Mentorship provides guidance, support, and knowledge transfer from experienced professionals to newcomers in the field. In IT, mentors help MCA graduates navigate career challenges, develop technical and soft skills, and build confidence. A strong mentor-mentee relationship accelerates learning, expands professional networks, and fosters innovation. Organizations that encourage mentorship cultivate talent, improve retention rates, and strengthen their workforce for long-term success.

43. Discuss the importance of confidentiality agreements in IT projects.
Answer: Confidentiality agreements protect sensitive information shared between parties during IT projects, ensuring it is not disclosed to unauthorized individuals. These agreements are vital for safeguarding client data, trade secrets, and intellectual property. For MCA graduates working on such projects, understanding and adhering to confidentiality clauses demonstrates professionalism and legal compliance. Upholding confidentiality builds trust with clients and minimizes risks of data breaches and reputational damage.

44. How can IT professionals ensure inclusivity in software design?
Answer: IT professionals ensure inclusivity by designing software that is accessible to diverse users, including those with disabilities or from varied cultural backgrounds. This involves implementing features like screen readers, multilingual support, and customizable interfaces. MCA graduates must follow accessibility standards such as WCAG and conduct usability testing with diverse user groups. Inclusive design promotes social equity, expands market reach, and aligns with ethical and legal obligations in software development.

45. Explain how professional etiquette contributes to a positive workplace culture.
Answer: Professional etiquette refers to appropriate behavior, communication, and interaction in the workplace. Practicing good etiquette—such as punctuality, respectful language, and active listening—fosters a harmonious environment. For MCA graduates entering corporate settings, etiquette ensures smooth collaboration, minimizes conflicts, and enhances their professional image. A culture of professionalism improves team morale, productivity, and retention, contributing to organizational success.

46. Discuss ethical concerns related to social media usage in professional life.
Answer: Social media raises ethical concerns such as data privacy breaches, sharing confidential company information, or engaging in inappropriate online behavior. IT professionals must balance personal expression with professional responsibilities, ensuring they do not damage their reputation or that of their employer. MCA graduates should adopt responsible social media practices, adhere to company policies, and be mindful of their digital footprint, as it can influence career opportunities and relationships.

47. What is professional accountability, and how does it affect teamwork?
Answer: Professional accountability means taking ownership of one's actions, decisions, and contributions in a team setting. It ensures that each member fulfills their responsibilities, meeting deadlines and maintaining quality standards. In IT teams, accountability fosters trust, reduces micromanagement, and encourages collaboration. MCA graduates who demonstrate accountability enhance team efficiency, strengthen relationships, and position themselves as reliable and valuable professionals.

48. Explain how ethics play a role in sustainable technology development.
Answer: Ethics guide sustainable technology development by ensuring innovations minimize environmental harm, use resources efficiently, and prioritize long-term societal benefits. For example, designing energy-efficient software or promoting green data centers reflects ethical responsibility. MCA graduates should consider sustainability in their work, aligning technical expertise with ethical principles to address global challenges like climate change while advancing technology responsibly.

49. Discuss the significance of professional certifications in upholding ethical standards.
Answer: Professional certifications often require adherence to ethical codes and standards as part of their credentialing process. Certifications like CISSP or PMP emphasize integrity, fairness, and responsibility in professional practice. MCA graduates pursuing certifications commit to these standards, reinforcing their reputation for ethical conduct. Such credentials demonstrate technical competence and ethical awareness, making certified professionals valuable assets to organizations seeking trustworthy employees.

50. How do IT professionals balance innovation with ethical considerations?
Answer: Balancing innovation with ethics involves developing cutting-edge technologies while ensuring they do not harm users, violate privacy, or reinforce inequalities. IT professionals must consider the societal impact of their solutions and implement safeguards against misuse. For MCA graduates, this balance requires critical thinking, adherence to ethical frameworks, and collaboration with diverse stakeholders. Ethical innovation fosters public trust, reduces risks, and contributes to sustainable technological progress.

51. Explain the role of transparency in building ethical IT organizations.
Answer: Transparency in IT organizations means openly sharing information about policies, processes, and decision-making with employees, clients, and stakeholders. It fosters trust by ensuring actions align with ethical and legal standards. For example, transparent communication about how user data is collected and used reassures clients about privacy. For MCA graduates, embracing transparency involves honesty in reporting progress, acknowledging mistakes, and maintaining open dialogue. Organizations that practice transparency reduce the risk of ethical violations and build long-term credibility in the competitive IT sector.

52. Discuss how ethical frameworks guide decision-making in professional environments.
Answer: Ethical frameworks provide structured approaches to evaluate choices and determine morally sound actions. Frameworks like utilitarianism (focusing on outcomes) and deontology (focusing on rules) help IT professionals analyze dilemmas such as balancing user privacy with business needs. For MCA graduates, understanding these

frameworks enables responsible decision-making that aligns with organizational values and societal expectations. Applying ethical frameworks ensures consistency in behavior and fosters a culture of accountability and fairness in professional environments.

53. What are the ethical challenges in outsourcing IT services?
Answer: Outsourcing IT services raises ethical challenges such as data privacy risks, exploitation of labor, and quality control concerns. For instance, transferring sensitive customer data to external vendors may expose it to unauthorized access. Cultural differences and unfair wages in outsourcing destinations can also lead to ethical conflicts. MCA graduates entering managerial roles should advocate for clear contracts, adherence to data protection regulations, and fair labor practices to ensure that outsourcing aligns with ethical standards.

54. Explain how critical thinking helps in addressing ethical dilemmas in IT.
Answer: Critical thinking equips IT professionals to analyze ethical dilemmas objectively, evaluate alternatives, and predict consequences. For instance, when handling user data, critical thinking helps assess whether business benefits outweigh potential privacy risks. MCA graduates who develop this skill can question assumptions, recognize biases, and make balanced decisions in alignment with professional codes of ethics. This approach fosters ethical innovation and prevents harmful practices that could damage organizational reputation or societal trust.

55. Discuss the significance of work-life balance in maintaining professional ethics.
Answer: Work-life balance is crucial for IT professionals to sustain productivity, creativity, and ethical judgment. Overwork often leads to stress, burnout, and poor decision-making, increasing the likelihood of ethical lapses like cutting corners or overlooking security protocols. MCA graduates who prioritize balance are more likely to act responsibly, respect organizational values, and deliver high-quality work. Organizations that support work-life balance foster a culture of ethical behavior and employee well-being.

56. How does confidentiality support ethical practices in software development?
Answer: Confidentiality ensures that sensitive information, such as source code, client data, and proprietary algorithms, is protected from unauthorized disclosure. Upholding confidentiality prevents misuse, safeguards intellectual property, and strengthens trust between IT professionals and stakeholders. For MCA graduates, maintaining confidentiality is a legal and ethical obligation, especially in projects involving healthcare, finance, or government data. Ethical practices in this regard prevent reputational and financial harm to organizations and clients.

57. Explain how interpersonal skills contribute to professional ethics.
Answer: Interpersonal skills like active listening, empathy, and respectful communication are integral to maintaining professional ethics. These skills enable IT professionals to collaborate effectively, resolve conflicts amicably, and understand diverse perspectives. For MCA graduates, strong interpersonal skills help in building trust with colleagues and clients, promoting an ethical work culture. They also reduce misunderstandings and foster a positive environment where ethical practices are valued and upheld.

58. Discuss the ethical concerns in cloud computing and data storage.
Answer: Cloud computing raises ethical concerns such as data security, user privacy, and compliance with jurisdictional laws. Storing data on third-party servers exposes it to breaches and unauthorized access. IT professionals must ensure encryption, secure access controls, and adherence to data protection laws like GDPR. MCA graduates should prioritize transparency with clients about cloud risks and implement robust safeguards to uphold ethical responsibilities while leveraging cloud technologies.

59. What is the role of self-discipline in professional ethics?
Answer: Self-discipline enables IT professionals to consistently adhere to ethical principles, even in challenging situations. It involves resisting shortcuts, avoiding unethical practices like plagiarism, and meeting commitments reliably. MCA graduates with strong self-discipline are more likely to uphold professional standards, earn trust, and set positive examples in their workplaces. This quality ensures long-term career success and contributes to a culture of integrity in organizations.

60. Explain how ethical behavior impacts organizational reputation in the IT sector.
Answer: Ethical behavior positively impacts organizational reputation by building trust among clients, partners, and employees. Companies known for ethical practices attract talent, retain customers, and gain competitive advantages. Conversely, unethical actions such as data breaches or software piracy can lead to legal penalties and reputational damage. MCA graduates entering the workforce play a key role in maintaining organizational integrity by adhering to ethical guidelines and advocating responsible practices.

61. Discuss the importance of ethical training programs for IT professionals.
Answer: Ethical training programs educate IT professionals on industry standards, legal obligations, and moral principles guiding their work. These programs raise awareness of issues like data privacy, intellectual property, and cybersecurity. For MCA graduates, participating in ethical training ensures they understand their responsibilities and can navigate complex dilemmas effectively. Organizations benefit from such programs by fostering a culture of accountability, reducing risks, and enhancing public trust in their services.

62. What are the ethical implications of workplace surveillance technologies?
Answer: Workplace surveillance technologies, such as monitoring emails or tracking productivity, raise ethical concerns about employee privacy and autonomy. While intended to enhance security or performance, excessive surveillance can erode trust and create hostile environments. MCA graduates in managerial positions should balance organizational needs with employee rights, implementing transparent policies and seeking informed consent to ensure ethical use of such technologies.

63. Explain the concept of social responsibility in the IT profession.
Answer: Social responsibility in IT involves using technology to benefit society while minimizing harm. This includes designing inclusive software, supporting environmental sustainability, and advocating for digital literacy. MCA graduates embracing social responsibility contribute positively to communities by developing solutions that address societal challenges, such as e-learning platforms or eco-friendly data centers. Socially responsible IT professionals ensure their innovations align with ethical values and promote long-term societal well-being.

64. Discuss the ethical considerations in developing algorithms for decision-making systems.
Answer: Algorithms used in decision-making systems, such as loan approvals or hiring tools, can perpetuate biases and discrimination if not designed carefully. Ethical considerations include fairness, transparency, accountability, and avoiding harm. MCA graduates working on such systems must ensure datasets are representative, audit algorithms for bias, and provide clear explanations of decisions to users. Ethical algorithm design fosters trust and prevents negative societal impacts from automated systems.

65. What is the significance of teamwork in upholding professional ethics?
Answer: Teamwork plays a vital role in upholding professional ethics by fostering accountability, collaboration, and mutual respect. In IT projects, ethical teams encourage open communication, share responsibilities fairly, and collectively address dilemmas. MCA graduates who value teamwork contribute to positive work cultures where ethical standards are maintained and reinforced. Collaborative environments also minimize unethical practices by promoting transparency and peer oversight.

66. How can IT professionals ensure ethical use of artificial intelligence?
Answer: IT professionals can ensure ethical AI use by incorporating fairness, transparency, and accountability into system design. This includes mitigating biases, providing explanations for AI decisions, and respecting user privacy. Ethical frameworks like "AI for Good" guide responsible innovation. MCA graduates entering AI fields must prioritize societal impacts, comply with regulations, and advocate ethical guidelines in organizations to prevent harm and promote equitable technology.

67. Discuss how emotional resilience supports ethical decision-making in high-pressure environments.
Answer: Emotional resilience helps professionals remain calm, focused, and principled under pressure. In high-stakes IT environments, it prevents rash or unethical choices driven by stress or fear. MCA graduates who cultivate resilience can navigate crises effectively, maintaining integrity and ethical standards even when facing tight deadlines or

challenging dilemmas. Resilient professionals contribute to stable, ethical work cultures and inspire confidence in their teams.

68. Explain the role of ethical considerations in intellectual property (IP) management.
Answer: Ethical IP management ensures that creators' rights are respected and innovations are not misappropriated. IT professionals must avoid plagiarism, adhere to licensing agreements, and protect confidential designs or algorithms. MCA graduates working with IP should understand copyright, patent, and open-source rules to ensure legal and ethical compliance. Proper IP management promotes innovation and trust in professional and academic settings.

69. What are the ethical concerns in developing persuasive technologies?
Answer: Persuasive technologies, such as apps designed to influence user behavior, raise ethical concerns about manipulation, addiction, and privacy. While beneficial for health campaigns or education, misuse for profit or political agendas can harm individuals and societies. MCA graduates must consider user autonomy and implement features like usage controls or transparency notices to ensure ethical deployment of persuasive systems.

70. Discuss how organizational leadership influences ethical culture in IT firms.
Answer: Organizational leadership shapes ethical culture by setting expectations, modeling integrity, and enforcing ethical standards. Leaders who prioritize ethics inspire employees to act responsibly and foster trust within and outside the organization. For MCA graduates aspiring to leadership roles, understanding this influence is crucial for building environments where ethical practices are integral to operations, innovation, and decision-making processes.

71. Explain the importance of ethical audits in IT organizations.
Answer: Ethical audits assess whether an organization's practices align with legal and moral standards, covering areas like data privacy, cybersecurity, and labor practices. These audits identify risks, ensure compliance, and reinforce accountability. MCA graduates contributing to ethical audits help organizations improve governance and maintain public trust, making audits an essential part of ethical IT management.

72. Discuss the role of ethical codes in professional associations like ACM or IEEE.
Answer: Ethical codes in professional associations like ACM and IEEE provide guidelines for responsible behavior and decision-making in technology fields. They emphasize principles such as honesty, fairness, and respect for user privacy. MCA graduates adhering to these codes align their professional conduct with industry standards, strengthening credibility and contributing to ethical advancements in IT.

73. How can IT professionals promote environmental sustainability in their work?
Answer: IT professionals promote sustainability by developing energy-efficient software, advocating green data centers, and supporting recycling of electronic waste. They can also design systems that reduce carbon footprints, such as teleconferencing tools to minimize travel. MCA graduates committed to environmental ethics ensure their work contributes to global sustainability efforts while advancing technology.

74. Explain the ethical responsibilities of IT professionals in combating cybercrime.
Answer: IT professionals have ethical responsibilities to design secure systems, educate users about threats, and collaborate with authorities to combat cybercrime. Neglecting security measures or exploiting vulnerabilities violates professional ethics. MCA graduates entering cybersecurity roles must act as ethical stewards, protecting systems and data while adhering to legal frameworks to deter cybercriminal activities.

75. Discuss how workplace diversity strengthens ethical practices in IT organizations.
Answer: Workplace diversity introduces varied perspectives and experiences, fostering inclusive decision-making and reducing biases in IT solutions. Diverse teams are better equipped to identify ethical risks and create technologies that serve broader user bases. For MCA graduates, embracing diversity strengthens collaboration and ensures their contributions reflect ethical sensitivity to different cultures and communities.

76. Explain how professional ethics influence decision-making in software engineering projects.
Answer: Professional ethics guide software engineers in making decisions that prioritize user safety, privacy, and fairness. Ethical decision-making ensures systems are designed responsibly, avoiding shortcuts that compromise

security or quality. For example, deciding whether to report a discovered vulnerability involves balancing company reputation and user safety. MCA graduates applying ethical principles consider the broader societal impact of their work, fostering trust and accountability. Ethical frameworks like ACM's code of ethics provide guidelines to navigate dilemmas and maintain professional integrity.

77. Discuss the ethical implications of using user data for targeted advertising.
Answer: Using user data for targeted advertising raises ethical concerns about privacy, consent, and manipulation. While personalization improves user experience, excessive data collection and opaque practices may breach trust. MCA graduates must ensure transparent data usage policies, obtain informed consent, and respect user autonomy. Balancing business objectives with ethical responsibility fosters sustainable practices that protect users and comply with legal standards such as GDPR.

78. What is corporate governance, and why is it important in IT organizations?
Answer: Corporate governance refers to the system of rules, practices, and processes that direct and control organizations. It ensures accountability, fairness, and transparency in decision-making. In IT, strong governance prevents unethical practices like data misuse or insider trading and supports compliance with legal frameworks. MCA graduates should understand governance structures as they contribute to ethical project management and organizational success. Ethical governance also boosts investor and customer confidence in the company.

79. Explain how continuous learning contributes to ethical professional growth.
Answer: Continuous learning helps professionals stay updated with technological advancements and ethical standards. In IT, new tools, frameworks, and regulations emerge rapidly, making learning essential. MCA graduates committed to learning can identify ethical risks in emerging technologies like AI or blockchain. This habit supports informed decision-making, reduces errors, and enables professionals to design solutions that align with societal needs and professional codes of conduct.

80. Discuss the role of ethical leadership in promoting workplace integrity.
Answer: Ethical leadership involves guiding teams with honesty, fairness, and a commitment to moral principles. Leaders set the tone for organizational behavior, ensuring integrity in operations and interactions. In IT, ethical leaders advocate secure coding practices, fair treatment of employees, and transparent decision-making. MCA graduates aspiring to leadership roles can inspire ethical cultures by modeling these behaviors, reducing misconduct, and fostering trust among stakeholders.

81. What are the ethical challenges of using open-source software in commercial projects?
Answer: Open-source software presents challenges such as licensing compliance, attribution obligations, and potential security risks. Using code without adhering to licenses like GPL or MIT can lead to legal disputes. MCA graduates must evaluate open-source components carefully, ensure proper crediting, and follow licensing terms. Ethical use of open-source fosters innovation while respecting contributors' efforts and avoiding misuse that could harm communities or businesses.

82. Explain how IT professionals can address biases in artificial intelligence systems.
Answer: Biases in AI arise from unrepresentative training data or flawed algorithms, leading to unfair outcomes. IT professionals must identify and mitigate these biases through diverse datasets, fairness audits, and inclusive design practices. MCA graduates should prioritize ethical AI development by ensuring transparency and explainability in models. Addressing biases not only enhances accuracy but also builds user trust and aligns with societal values of equality and fairness.

83. Discuss the significance of ethical outsourcing practices in global IT projects.
Answer: Ethical outsourcing involves fair labor practices, data protection, and respect for cultural differences. Organizations must ensure outsourced teams receive equitable compensation and operate under ethical working conditions. MCA graduates managing global projects should promote clear contracts, compliance with local laws, and secure data handling. Ethical outsourcing builds trust, strengthens client relationships, and enhances the reputation of IT organizations in international markets.

84. What is the role of intellectual honesty in academic and professional IT work?
Answer: Intellectual honesty requires acknowledging sources, presenting accurate data, and avoiding plagiarism or misrepresentation. In academia, it ensures fair evaluation and contributes to knowledge advancement. In IT professions, it underpins credibility and ethical decision-making. MCA graduates must practice intellectual honesty by citing open-source libraries, documenting work properly, and giving credit where due. Upholding this principle builds a foundation of trust and integrity in both academic and workplace environments.

85. Explain how cybersecurity professionals balance ethics and legal obligations.
Answer: Cybersecurity professionals must balance ethics and legal obligations by protecting systems while respecting privacy and avoiding overreach. Ethical considerations include obtaining consent for penetration testing and refraining from exploiting vulnerabilities for personal gain. Legal frameworks like GDPR guide acceptable practices. MCA graduates in cybersecurity roles must act responsibly, ensuring compliance with laws while upholding ethical standards to prevent harm and foster digital trust.

86. Discuss how cultural awareness supports ethical global collaborations in IT.
Answer: Cultural awareness involves understanding and respecting diverse cultural norms, values, and communication styles. In global IT projects, it minimizes misunderstandings and fosters ethical interactions. MCA graduates working in multicultural teams can adapt to varied expectations, promote inclusivity, and avoid decisions that unintentionally disrespect cultural sensitivities. Cultural awareness enhances collaboration, builds stronger relationships, and ensures ethical conduct across borders.

87. What are the ethical considerations in software testing and quality assurance?
Answer: Ethical considerations in testing include honesty in reporting bugs, avoiding negligence, and prioritizing user safety. Cutting corners in testing can result in faulty systems and harm end users. MCA graduates must adopt rigorous quality assurance practices, document results transparently, and advocate for sufficient testing time. Upholding testing ethics prevents reputational damage and ensures reliable, secure software delivery.

88. Explain how digital literacy contributes to ethical IT practices.
Answer: Digital literacy equips professionals with the knowledge to use technology responsibly and understand its societal impact. It helps MCA graduates recognize ethical issues like misinformation, data privacy, and cybersecurity risks. Promoting digital literacy within organizations and communities empowers users to make informed decisions, reducing unethical behaviors like piracy or unsafe online practices. Ethical IT practices thrive when professionals and users are digitally literate.

89. Discuss how ethical principles guide the design of accessible technologies.
Answer: Ethical principles like inclusivity and fairness guide the design of technologies that cater to users with diverse needs. Accessibility features, such as screen readers or keyboard navigation, ensure equitable participation for individuals with disabilities. MCA graduates developing software must follow standards like WCAG and conduct user testing with diverse groups. Ethical design improves user experience, meets legal requirements, and reflects social responsibility in the IT industry.

90. What are the ethical implications of artificial intelligence in decision-making for healthcare systems?
Answer: AI in healthcare raises ethical concerns about accuracy, transparency, and accountability. Misdiagnoses due to algorithmic flaws can endanger lives. MCA graduates involved in healthcare AI must prioritize patient safety, ensure models are explainable, and involve medical professionals in development. Ethical AI deployment supports informed decisions, protects privacy, and aligns with principles like beneficence and non-maleficence in healthcare ethics.

91. Explain how mentorship programs promote ethical professional development.
Answer: Mentorship programs promote ethical growth by guiding young professionals in navigating workplace challenges and dilemmas. Experienced mentors instill values like integrity, accountability, and respect. MCA graduates participating as mentees gain insights into ethical practices and decision-making frameworks. Organizations benefit from mentorship by fostering a culture of learning and ethical conduct that supports long-term success.

92. Discuss the role of transparency in ethical software development lifecycles.
Answer: Transparency ensures that stakeholders are informed about project progress, risks, and decisions. In ethical software development, it involves clear documentation, open communication about limitations, and user-friendly privacy policies. MCA graduates working on teams should advocate for transparent workflows to prevent misunderstandings and foster trust among clients and team members. Transparency promotes accountability and ethical alignment in every phase of the development lifecycle.

93. What are the ethical concerns surrounding big data analytics?
Answer: Big data analytics involves processing massive datasets, raising ethical concerns like user consent, surveillance, and data misuse. MCA graduates must ensure anonymization of data, obtain explicit permissions, and avoid discriminatory outcomes in analytics. Ethical practices balance business insights with individual rights, fostering trust in data-driven solutions and complying with global privacy regulations.

94. Explain how conflict of interest can arise in IT projects and how to manage it ethically.
Answer: A conflict of interest occurs when personal interests could compromise professional judgment. In IT, this might involve favoring vendors due to personal relationships or misusing insider information. MCA graduates should disclose potential conflicts, recuse themselves from biased decisions, and adhere to organizational policies. Ethical management prevents reputational harm and ensures fair project outcomes.

95. Discuss how emotional intelligence supports ethical leadership in IT teams.
Answer: Emotional intelligence (EI) enables leaders to understand and manage emotions effectively, fostering ethical decision-making and conflict resolution. IT leaders with high EI can empathize with team members, encourage open communication, and navigate stressful situations with integrity. MCA graduates developing EI strengthen their ability to lead ethically, inspiring teams to uphold professional standards and collaborate productively.

96. What is the role of ethical standards in designing autonomous systems?
Answer: Ethical standards in autonomous systems ensure decisions align with societal values, prioritizing safety and fairness. For example, self-driving cars must balance efficiency with ethical considerations in accident scenarios. MCA graduates designing such systems should implement transparency, human oversight, and compliance with regulatory frameworks to prevent harm and promote trust in autonomous technologies.

97. Explain the importance of ethical innovation in disruptive technologies.
Answer: Disruptive technologies like blockchain or AI challenge existing norms, requiring careful ethical consideration. Ethical innovation ensures these technologies address real-world problems without creating unintended harm. MCA graduates can drive ethical innovation by engaging stakeholders, assessing societal impact, and embedding fairness into designs. Responsible innovation balances progress with accountability and public trust.

98. Discuss how IT professionals can promote digital well-being among users.
Answer: IT professionals promote digital well-being by designing tools that encourage balanced usage, such as screen time monitors or focus modes. MCA graduates can advocate ethical design practices that reduce addictive patterns and prioritize user mental health. Promoting digital well-being aligns with corporate social responsibility and enhances user loyalty to products.

99. What are the ethical responsibilities of IT consultants in client relationships?
Answer: IT consultants have ethical responsibilities to provide honest advice, protect client confidentiality, and avoid conflicts of interest. Misrepresenting expertise or recommending unnecessary solutions violates professional ethics. MCA graduates entering consultancy roles should prioritize transparency and fairness, ensuring long-term trust and successful client partnerships.

100. Explain how workplace ethics influence organizational sustainability in IT firms.
Answer: Workplace ethics promote transparency, fairness, and social responsibility, which are vital for organizational sustainability. Ethical firms attract talent, retain customers, and adapt better to regulatory changes. MCA graduates practicing workplace ethics contribute to positive cultures that support innovation and resilience, ensuring IT firms thrive in the long term.

101. Explain how ethical considerations impact cybersecurity policies in organizations.
Answer: Ethical considerations shape cybersecurity policies by ensuring they respect user privacy, transparency, and fairness. Policies must balance protecting organizational assets with employee rights, avoiding invasive practices like excessive monitoring. MCA graduates working in cybersecurity must design policies that adhere to legal frameworks such as GDPR and foster trust among stakeholders. Ethical cybersecurity policies also promote proactive measures, such as educating employees about threats and responsibly handling vulnerabilities, which safeguard both organizations and users in the digital ecosystem.

102. Discuss how diversity and inclusion influence ethical practices in IT workplaces.
Answer: Diversity and inclusion create environments where varied perspectives contribute to fairer decision-making and innovation. Ethical practices flourish in inclusive IT workplaces as discrimination is minimized and equitable opportunities are provided. MCA graduates can promote inclusivity by collaborating with colleagues from diverse backgrounds and designing technologies that cater to all users. Diversity in teams also reduces the likelihood of biased algorithms and enhances creativity, strengthening the ethical foundation of organizations.

103. What is ethical consumerism, and how does it relate to IT products and services?
Answer: Ethical consumerism involves choosing products and services based on their environmental, social, and ethical impact. In IT, this means preferring companies that respect user privacy, adopt sustainable practices, and avoid exploitative labor. MCA graduates can contribute by developing software and systems that align with ethical consumer expectations, such as energy-efficient applications or platforms with transparent data usage policies. Supporting ethical consumerism builds trust and aligns IT innovation with societal values.

104. Explain how conflict management contributes to professional ethics.
Answer: Conflict management fosters ethical workplaces by resolving disagreements constructively and ensuring fairness. In IT teams, conflicts may arise from competing priorities or cultural differences. MCA graduates with strong conflict management skills listen empathetically, mediate discussions, and guide parties towards mutually beneficial solutions. Ethical conflict resolution maintains team cohesion, reduces workplace stress, and promotes a respectful environment where collaboration and innovation thrive.

105. Discuss the significance of ethical considerations in mobile application development.
Answer: Mobile app development involves ethical considerations such as protecting user data, preventing addiction, and ensuring accessibility. Poorly designed apps may compromise privacy through unnecessary permissions or exploit users with manipulative design patterns. MCA graduates should follow ethical guidelines, use secure coding practices, and implement features like privacy dashboards. Ethical apps enhance user trust and comply with regulations, creating sustainable and responsible technology ecosystems.

106. How does workplace ethics influence employee retention in IT companies?
Answer: Workplace ethics, characterized by fairness, transparency, and respect, significantly impact employee retention. Ethical companies provide supportive environments where employees feel valued and motivated. MCA graduates in managerial roles can contribute by promoting open communication, recognizing achievements, and addressing grievances promptly. Organizations with strong ethical cultures experience lower turnover, attract top talent, and foster long-term loyalty, ensuring stability and growth.

107. Explain how ethical decision-making affects the success of IT startups.
Answer: Ethical decision-making is crucial for IT startups as it builds trust among investors, customers, and employees. Startups often face pressures to cut corners, but maintaining ethical practices ensures sustainable growth. MCA graduates working in startups must prioritize transparency, respect user rights, and comply with regulations. Ethical foundations attract partnerships and prevent legal issues, positioning startups for long-term success in competitive markets.

108. What are the ethical challenges in implementing Internet of Things (IoT) systems?
Answer: IoT systems present challenges like data privacy, security vulnerabilities, and consent management. Devices continuously collect and transmit user data, raising concerns about misuse or unauthorized access. MCA graduates developing IoT solutions must design secure architectures, implement encryption, and provide clear privacy policies.

Addressing these ethical challenges protects users and enhances trust in IoT technologies as they integrate further into daily life.

109. Discuss the role of ethics in building artificial intelligence systems for education.
Answer: Ethics in AI for education ensures fairness, inclusivity, and privacy. Algorithms must avoid biases that disadvantage certain student groups and respect the confidentiality of student data. MCA graduates developing such systems should focus on transparency, provide human oversight, and prioritize educational equity. Ethical AI in education empowers learners while supporting teachers in delivering personalized, responsible, and effective learning experiences.

110. Explain how corporate social responsibility (CSR) aligns with IT professional ethics.
Answer: CSR initiatives align with professional ethics by extending organizational responsibility beyond profits to include societal and environmental impacts. IT companies engage in CSR by supporting digital literacy, reducing e-waste, or developing eco-friendly technologies. MCA graduates can participate in CSR efforts, reflecting their commitment to ethical values. CSR strengthens organizational reputation, fosters public trust, and creates positive societal change while encouraging ethical practices within teams.

111. Discuss how ethical leadership impacts decision-making in IT project teams.
Answer: Ethical leadership ensures that IT project decisions prioritize fairness, transparency, and accountability. Leaders who model integrity influence team members to adopt similar standards, fostering cohesive and ethical workflows. MCA graduates in leadership roles can set clear expectations, encourage open dialogue, and ensure decisions align with both organizational goals and societal values. Ethical leadership reduces conflicts and enhances the success of IT projects.

112. What are the ethical responsibilities of IT professionals in protecting user privacy?
Answer: IT professionals are responsible for designing systems that safeguard user privacy through encryption, access controls, and transparent policies. MCA graduates working in data-intensive fields must minimize data collection, obtain informed consent, and prevent unauthorized sharing. Upholding privacy not only ensures legal compliance but also builds user trust, which is critical for long-term success in the digital world.

113. Explain how ethical considerations shape the use of biometric technologies.
Answer: Biometric technologies, such as facial recognition and fingerprint scanning, raise concerns about surveillance, consent, and data security. Ethical considerations require IT professionals to implement safeguards against misuse, prevent discrimination, and ensure transparency in how biometric data is stored and processed. MCA graduates should follow regulatory guidelines and prioritize user rights to prevent ethical breaches that could harm public trust.

114. Discuss the role of ethical frameworks in designing blockchain solutions.
Answer: Blockchain offers transparency and decentralization but also poses ethical risks like misuse for illicit activities and energy consumption. Ethical frameworks guide IT professionals in balancing innovation with societal impact. MCA graduates can design blockchain systems that promote fairness, such as inclusive financial solutions or eco-friendly consensus algorithms. Applying ethical principles ensures blockchain serves as a positive force in industries and communities.

115. How does ethical behavior in IT enhance client relationships?
Answer: Ethical behavior, such as honesty, confidentiality, and reliability, strengthens client relationships by fostering trust and satisfaction. MCA graduates entering client-facing roles must deliver on commitments, communicate transparently, and avoid misrepresentation. Ethical interactions build loyalty and establish long-term partnerships, which are crucial for the success of IT service providers in competitive markets.

116. Explain the ethical implications of using predictive analytics in healthcare.
Answer: Predictive analytics in healthcare raises ethical concerns about accuracy, bias, and patient privacy. Inaccurate predictions can lead to misdiagnoses, while biased algorithms may disadvantage certain populations. MCA graduates

developing these systems must ensure data quality, fairness, and compliance with healthcare regulations. Ethical practices ensure patient safety, promote equitable care, and strengthen trust in data-driven healthcare innovations.

117. Discuss how emotional intelligence helps IT professionals manage ethical dilemmas.
Answer: Emotional intelligence (EI) enables professionals to understand emotions, empathize with stakeholders, and navigate ethical dilemmas calmly. In IT, EI helps MCA graduates recognize the human impact of decisions, balance competing interests, and maintain integrity under pressure. Developing EI supports ethical reasoning, fostering collaborative and responsible solutions in challenging workplace scenarios.

118. What are the ethical challenges in implementing surveillance technologies?
Answer: Surveillance technologies raise privacy, consent, and misuse concerns. Excessive monitoring can infringe on individual freedoms and create mistrust. MCA graduates working on such systems must design with transparency, allow opt-out options, and ensure data is used solely for legitimate purposes. Ethical approaches balance security needs with respect for civil liberties.

119. Explain the importance of ethical guidelines in workplace technology use.
Answer: Ethical guidelines ensure that workplace technology is used responsibly, protecting data security and employee privacy. Policies may cover acceptable internet use, software licensing, and handling of sensitive information. MCA graduates following these guidelines reduce risks of breaches, legal issues, and ethical violations, contributing to a safe and productive work environment.

120. Discuss the ethical considerations in developing persuasive user interfaces.
Answer: Persuasive interfaces, such as gamification or notifications, aim to influence user behavior but may risk manipulation or addiction. MCA graduates must ensure such designs respect user autonomy and promote positive outcomes, like encouraging healthy habits. Ethical UI design builds user trust and prevents exploitative practices that harm well-being.

Chapter 7: Most Asked Questions Part-B

1. Analyze how an IT professional should handle a situation where they discover a major security flaw in their company's product.

Answer: When an IT professional discovers a major security flaw, ethical responsibility requires them to report it promptly to relevant authorities within the organization, such as the security or development team. They must avoid public disclosure or exploiting the flaw, as it could harm users or damage the company's reputation. Documenting the issue clearly and suggesting potential fixes demonstrates professionalism. If management ignores the vulnerability and it poses a public risk, ethical frameworks may justify whistleblowing through legal channels. MCA graduates must follow company policies and prioritize user safety, maintaining integrity throughout the process.

2. Discuss how cultural diversity in global IT teams influences professional behavior and ethics.

Answer: Cultural diversity in global IT teams brings varied perspectives, but also requires sensitivity to different ethical norms and communication styles. Professionals must avoid stereotypes, respect cultural differences, and adapt their behavior to promote inclusivity. For MCA graduates, understanding diversity ensures ethical collaboration, minimizes misunderstandings, and strengthens team cohesion. Ethical training programs can help teams navigate cultural nuances, ensuring fair decision-making and fostering an environment where all members contribute meaningfully to global IT projects.

3. Evaluate the ethical implications of implementing AI surveillance in public spaces.

Answer: AI surveillance in public spaces raises ethical concerns about privacy, consent, and potential misuse. While it can enhance security, it risks creating a surveillance society where individuals feel constantly monitored. MCA graduates involved in such projects must ensure transparency, implement strict data protection measures, and provide citizens with information about how data is collected and used. Ethical frameworks suggest balancing public safety with individual freedoms, avoiding overreach, and complying with laws to maintain trust in technology deployment.

4. How should IT consultants ethically manage conflicts of interest with their clients?

Answer: IT consultants must disclose any potential conflicts of interest, such as partnerships with competitors or financial incentives that could bias their advice. Ethical management involves recusing themselves from decisions where impartiality is compromised and prioritizing the client's best interests. MCA graduates entering consultancy roles should adhere to professional codes of conduct and maintain transparency to build long-term trust and credibility with clients. This approach fosters fairness and prevents reputational harm for both the consultant and the organization.

5. Analyze the role of ethical leadership in preventing workplace discrimination in IT firms.

Answer: Ethical leaders model fairness and enforce policies that promote equality, ensuring hiring, promotions, and project assignments are free from discrimination. They create safe environments for employees to voice concerns and implement training programs to raise awareness about unconscious biases. For MCA graduates aspiring to leadership, practicing ethical leadership means valuing diversity, addressing grievances promptly, and fostering an inclusive culture where all employees can thrive, ultimately enhancing organizational performance and reputation.

6. Explain how IT professionals can balance innovation with ethical concerns in developing addictive technologies.

Answer: While innovative technologies like social media and gaming apps drive engagement, they can lead to user addiction if not designed responsibly. MCA graduates must consider ethical implications by implementing features like usage limits, reminders, and parental controls. Transparent communication about addictive elements and promoting digital well-being align business goals with societal responsibilities. Balancing innovation with ethics ensures sustainable user engagement and protects the company from criticism or regulatory backlash.

7. Discuss the ethical considerations in outsourcing IT projects to countries with different labor laws.

Answer: Outsourcing to countries with weaker labor protections raises concerns about fair wages, working conditions, and exploitation. MCA graduates managing such projects should advocate for ethical outsourcing practices, including auditing vendors for compliance with labor standards and ensuring transparency in contracts. Ethical considerations also involve protecting client data across borders and respecting cultural differences. Prioritizing fair practices builds trust with stakeholders and strengthens the global IT ecosystem.

8. Evaluate how IT professionals should respond if asked to participate in unethical practices like data manipulation.
Answer: IT professionals have an ethical obligation to refuse participation in data manipulation, which undermines trust and can have legal consequences. MCA graduates faced with such requests should escalate concerns to higher management or ethics committees and document their refusal to protect themselves. If internal channels fail, they may need to report externally under whistleblower protections. Upholding professional integrity safeguards the individual's career and supports the organization's long-term credibility.

9. Analyze the ethical impact of using facial recognition technology in schools.
Answer: Using facial recognition in schools raises ethical questions about student privacy, consent, and potential biases in the technology. MCA graduates developing such systems must ensure transparency with parents and students, secure data storage, and compliance with privacy laws. Ethical deployment requires evaluating whether the benefits, such as enhanced security, outweigh risks to civil liberties and considering alternatives that are less intrusive.

10. Discuss how professional networking platforms like LinkedIn raise ethical issues for IT professionals.
Answer: Professional networking platforms collect and share vast amounts of personal data, raising ethical concerns about privacy and consent. IT professionals using these platforms must protect their organization's confidential information and avoid inappropriate conduct online. MCA graduates should maintain professionalism, verify the accuracy of their shared credentials, and understand platform policies to prevent misuse. Ethical engagement strengthens their personal brand while contributing positively to the professional community.

11. How can IT professionals promote ethical behavior in open-source development communities?
Answer: Open-source communities thrive on collaboration, but ethical issues like plagiarism, lack of attribution, and toxic behavior can arise. MCA graduates can promote ethics by respecting licenses, crediting contributors, and fostering inclusive environments. Enforcing community guidelines and addressing conflicts respectfully maintains trust and encourages sustainable contributions to open-source projects.

12. Evaluate the ethical dilemmas faced when developing autonomous vehicles.
Answer: Autonomous vehicle developers face dilemmas such as decision-making in unavoidable accident scenarios (e.g., protecting passengers vs. pedestrians). MCA graduates working in this field must prioritize safety, transparency in algorithm design, and regulatory compliance. Engaging ethicists and diverse stakeholders in design processes ensures these systems reflect societal values and minimize harm in complex situations.

13. Discuss the ethical responsibilities of IT professionals in managing fake news on digital platforms.
Answer: IT professionals designing or maintaining digital platforms have a responsibility to combat the spread of fake news. This involves implementing verification systems, flagging mechanisms, and educating users about reliable sources. MCA graduates must balance freedom of speech with public safety, ensuring interventions are transparent and unbiased to maintain trust in platforms.

14. Explain how data localization laws create ethical challenges for global IT companies.
Answer: Data localization laws require storing user data within national borders, raising ethical issues about user privacy and cross-border innovation. MCA graduates working in global firms must balance compliance with local laws while advocating ethical practices, such as minimizing surveillance risks and maintaining user trust. Transparent communication about how and where data is stored is critical to navigate these challenges responsibly.

15. Analyze the importance of whistleblower protection policies in IT organizations.
Answer: Whistleblower protection encourages employees to report unethical practices like fraud or data breaches without fear of retaliation. MCA graduates should support such policies by fostering awareness and ensuring secure reporting mechanisms. Ethical organizations that protect whistleblowers demonstrate accountability, reduce misconduct, and enhance their credibility with stakeholders.

16. Evaluate how IT professionals should address ethical concerns in developing persuasive technologies.
Answer: Persuasive technologies, such as social media platforms and mobile apps, aim to influence user behavior. While beneficial for promoting positive habits, they risk encouraging addiction or manipulative practices. IT

professionals must adopt ethical design principles like transparency, informed consent, and user control. MCA graduates developing such systems should ensure features like time reminders and parental controls promote healthy usage. Balancing engagement with user well-being reflects corporate social responsibility and prevents ethical and legal repercussions.

17. Discuss the ethical considerations in implementing employee monitoring software in IT organizations.
Answer: Employee monitoring software raises ethical concerns about privacy, consent, and trust. While organizations use it to improve productivity and security, excessive surveillance can create stress and harm workplace morale. MCA graduates managing such tools should ensure transparency by informing employees about monitoring policies and using data responsibly. Ethical practices involve balancing organizational needs with respect for employee autonomy and complying with data protection laws.

18. How should IT project managers ethically handle delays in project delivery?
Answer: When facing project delays, IT project managers must act ethically by communicating honestly with stakeholders and providing realistic timelines. Covering up delays or compromising on quality undermines trust and can damage reputations. MCA graduates in management roles should analyze the causes, propose corrective measures, and prioritize transparency. Ethical handling fosters client confidence and strengthens long-term professional relationships, even in challenging circumstances.

19. Analyze the ethical impact of algorithmic decision-making in financial systems.
Answer: Algorithmic decision-making in financial systems introduces risks like bias, lack of transparency, and potential exclusion of marginalized groups. Ethical IT professionals must ensure algorithms are fair, explainable, and subject to regular audits. MCA graduates designing such systems should prioritize user rights and compliance with financial regulations to prevent harm. Addressing these concerns upholds public trust and ensures equitable access to financial services.

20. Discuss how IT professionals can ensure ethical practices in cloud computing environments.
Answer: Ethical practices in cloud computing involve safeguarding data privacy, ensuring security, and maintaining transparency about how user data is stored and processed. IT professionals must comply with regulations like GDPR and ensure clients understand risks and responsibilities. MCA graduates working in cloud systems should advocate encryption, secure access controls, and ethical vendor selection. These measures protect sensitive information and foster user confidence in cloud-based solutions.

21. Evaluate the role of ethical considerations in designing e-learning platforms.
Answer: E-learning platforms must consider ethics to ensure accessibility, data privacy, and equitable opportunities for learners. Challenges include protecting minors' data, preventing bias in content delivery, and promoting digital well-being. MCA graduates developing such systems should adhere to global accessibility standards, implement parental controls, and design features that encourage healthy learning habits. Ethical considerations support inclusivity and help build trust with educational institutions and learners.

22. Explain how IT professionals should handle ethical dilemmas involving intellectual property in software development.
Answer: Ethical dilemmas around intellectual property (IP) often involve unauthorized use or misattribution of code and designs. IT professionals should respect licensing agreements, credit original creators, and avoid plagiarism. MCA graduates working on collaborative projects should verify open-source licenses and consult legal teams to ensure compliance. Ethical IP management fosters innovation, avoids legal disputes, and upholds professional integrity in software development.

23. Discuss the ethical challenges in implementing biometric authentication systems.
Answer: Biometric systems, like fingerprint or facial recognition, raise ethical issues related to consent, data storage, and misuse. Breaches can expose highly sensitive personal data. MCA graduates designing these systems must prioritize encryption, secure storage, and clear user consent policies. Addressing potential biases in recognition algorithms is also crucial to prevent discrimination. Ethical implementation safeguards user rights and builds trust in advanced authentication technologies.

24. How should IT professionals approach ethical decision-making in high-pressure environments?
Answer: High-pressure environments can tempt professionals to compromise ethics for speed or cost savings. IT professionals must adhere to core ethical principles, even under stress, and prioritize long-term consequences over short-term gains. MCA graduates should apply critical thinking, consult stakeholders, and use ethical frameworks to guide their decisions. Upholding integrity during challenging situations strengthens reputations and prevents risks that could harm the organization or users.

25. Analyze the ethical considerations in designing technologies for vulnerable populations.
Answer: Technologies for vulnerable populations, such as children, the elderly, or people with disabilities, require heightened ethical sensitivity. Risks include privacy violations, exploitation, or exclusion due to poor design. MCA graduates must ensure these systems are inclusive, accessible, and secure. Engaging with stakeholders from these groups during development promotes ethical design that empowers users rather than creating dependencies or harm.

26. Explain how IT professionals should ethically manage user data in mobile applications.
Answer: Managing user data ethically requires IT professionals to collect only necessary information, obtain explicit consent, and maintain transparency about data usage. Mobile apps often access sensitive information like location or contacts, making privacy paramount. MCA graduates developing apps should implement robust encryption, allow users to control permissions, and comply with privacy regulations such as GDPR. Ethical data management fosters trust and protects users from potential misuse or breaches.

27. Discuss the ethical challenges of designing AI algorithms for hiring processes.
Answer: AI hiring algorithms can inadvertently perpetuate biases if trained on non-representative data, leading to unfair treatment of candidates. Ethical challenges include transparency in decision-making, explaining rejections, and ensuring equal opportunities for diverse groups. MCA graduates must design systems with fairness audits, eliminate discriminatory patterns, and provide human oversight. Ethical hiring AI enhances organizational diversity and maintains public confidence in technology-assisted recruitment.

28. Analyze how IT professionals can ensure ethical use of location tracking in applications.
Answer: Location tracking can enhance user experiences but raises privacy concerns if misused or collected without consent. IT professionals should seek explicit user permission, provide opt-out options, and avoid sharing data with third parties without disclosure. MCA graduates must also ensure secure storage of location data and minimize its retention. Ethical location tracking balances functionality with user autonomy and complies with privacy laws.

29. Explain the ethical responsibilities of IT professionals in addressing software piracy.
Answer: Software piracy undermines intellectual property rights and discourages innovation. IT professionals have an ethical responsibility to use and promote licensed software, educate users about legal alternatives, and implement piracy prevention mechanisms in their products. MCA graduates must lead by example, discouraging piracy in their workplaces and advocating for open-source solutions when appropriate to balance access with ethics.

30. Discuss how ethical frameworks guide IT professionals in resolving conflicts during global projects.
Answer: Global IT projects involve diverse teams and stakeholders, often leading to ethical conflicts over cultural practices, resource allocation, or priorities. Ethical frameworks like utilitarianism or deontology help professionals evaluate choices objectively and seek fair resolutions. MCA graduates can use these frameworks to align decisions with organizational values, ensuring respect for cultural differences and fostering collaboration in international teams.

31. Evaluate how IT professionals can prevent misuse of deepfake technology.
Answer: Deepfake technology poses risks of misinformation, harassment, and identity theft. IT professionals must implement ethical safeguards, such as watermarks, detection tools, and user education about responsible use. MCA graduates developing or working with such technology should advocate for regulations, restrict access for harmful purposes, and design systems that prioritize authenticity and accountability in digital media.

32. Explain the role of ethics in designing health monitoring wearable devices.
Answer: Wearable devices collect sensitive health data, requiring ethical handling to protect privacy and ensure accuracy. IT professionals must implement secure data storage, obtain informed consent, and provide users with clear

insights into how their data is used. MCA graduates working on such devices should also consider inclusivity, ensuring wearables accommodate diverse users without bias. Ethical designs promote user safety, trust, and regulatory compliance in healthcare technologies.

33. Discuss the ethical considerations in designing gamified learning platforms for children.
Answer: Gamified platforms for children must prioritize safety, avoid manipulative tactics, and respect age-appropriate content guidelines. Ethical concerns include data privacy, preventing addiction, and ensuring equitable access. MCA graduates developing such systems should follow child protection regulations like COPPA and design features that encourage learning rather than exploiting attention. Ethical design supports positive educational outcomes and builds trust with parents and educators.

34. Analyze how IT professionals can address ethical concerns in predictive policing technologies.
Answer: Predictive policing uses algorithms to forecast crime hotspots, but it raises concerns about racial profiling, data bias, and privacy violations. IT professionals must ensure transparency in how predictions are made and involve communities in oversight. MCA graduates working on such systems should advocate fairness audits, avoid reinforcing societal inequalities, and comply with ethical guidelines to balance safety with civil liberties.

35. Explain how ethical practices influence client trust in IT consultancy services.
Answer: Ethical practices like honesty, confidentiality, and transparency build strong client relationships in consultancy. Misleading clients or failing to disclose risks erodes trust and harms reputations. MCA graduates in consultancy roles must prioritize the client's best interests, avoid conflicts of interest, and communicate clearly about solutions. Consistent ethical conduct fosters long-term partnerships and enhances credibility in competitive IT markets.

36. Discuss the ethical responsibilities of IT professionals in combating misinformation on social media.
Answer: Social media platforms often spread misinformation, impacting public opinion and safety. IT professionals have a duty to design systems that detect and mitigate false content, promote reliable sources, and respect free speech. MCA graduates working in this domain should balance content moderation with transparency and user education, ensuring interventions are fair and ethical.

37. Evaluate how ethical decision-making affects the success of IT startups.
Answer: Ethical decision-making in startups fosters trust among investors, customers, and employees, crucial for long-term success. Startups often face pressures to compromise ethics for rapid growth, but maintaining integrity ensures sustainability. MCA graduates in startups should prioritize user privacy, fair employment practices, and compliance with regulations. Ethical foundations help startups avoid legal issues and attract responsible stakeholders.

38. Explain how IT professionals can ensure fairness in algorithmic loan approval systems.
Answer: Algorithmic loan systems risk bias against certain demographics if trained on skewed data. IT professionals must ensure datasets are diverse, implement fairness metrics, and allow human oversight in critical decisions. MCA graduates working on such systems should design with transparency and provide explanations for loan approvals or rejections. Ethical practices ensure financial inclusion and uphold user trust.

39. Discuss the ethical implications of using AI chatbots in mental health support.
Answer: AI chatbots in mental health offer accessibility but pose ethical concerns about accuracy, data privacy, and lack of human empathy. MCA graduates developing such tools must clearly communicate their limitations, ensure user data security, and design escalation features for emergencies. Ethical implementation enhances user safety while complementing professional mental health services.

40. Analyze how workplace ethics influence innovation in IT companies.
Answer: Ethical workplaces encourage innovation by fostering trust, collaboration, and psychological safety. Employees in such environments feel empowered to share ideas without fear of exploitation or bias. MCA graduates contributing to ethical cultures promote sustainable innovation that balances creativity with responsibility, ensuring products align with societal values and organizational integrity.

41. Explain how IT professionals can design ethical recommender systems for e-commerce platforms.
Answer: Recommender systems must avoid manipulative practices like promoting addictive purchases or exploiting user data. IT professionals should ensure recommendations are transparent, respect user privacy, and allow customization of preferences. MCA graduates can advocate ethical designs that prioritize user benefit over solely maximizing profits, building customer trust and loyalty.

42. Discuss the ethical considerations in designing virtual reality (VR) environments.
Answer: VR environments raise concerns about user safety, psychological effects, and data privacy. IT professionals must design age-appropriate content, prevent harassment in virtual spaces, and secure user data. MCA graduates should consider accessibility for diverse users and avoid addictive or harmful VR experiences, ensuring technology enhances well-being rather than causing harm.

43. Evaluate how IT professionals should respond to clients requesting unethical software features.
Answer: When clients request unethical features, such as spyware or discriminatory algorithms, IT professionals must refuse and explain the legal and ethical implications. MCA graduates should offer alternative solutions that meet client goals without compromising ethics. Escalating concerns internally or withdrawing from the project may be necessary to maintain professional integrity.

44. Explain the ethical challenges in integrating AI with autonomous weapons systems.
Answer: Integrating AI into weapons systems raises serious ethical concerns about accountability, unintended consequences, and loss of human control. MCA graduates working in defense technologies must advocate for strict regulations, transparency, and human oversight in deployment decisions. Ethical frameworks suggest prioritizing humanitarian principles to prevent harm.

45. Discuss how IT professionals can promote sustainable practices in software engineering.
Answer: Sustainable software engineering involves optimizing code for energy efficiency, reducing server loads, and supporting eco-friendly hardware. IT professionals should consider environmental impacts at every stage of development. MCA graduates can champion green coding practices and advocate organizational policies that reduce the carbon footprint of IT operations.

46. Analyze how ethical guidelines support IT professionals in handling sensitive government data.
Answer: Handling government data requires adherence to strict ethical standards, including confidentiality, security, and compliance with laws. MCA graduates in such roles must avoid unauthorized disclosures and ensure systems are resilient against cyberattacks. Ethical conduct ensures public trust and prevents national security risks.

47. Explain how IT professionals should ethically manage user feedback in system improvements.
Answer: User feedback is critical for improvements but must be handled ethically by respecting privacy and avoiding manipulation. IT professionals should seek consent when analyzing feedback data and ensure transparency about how suggestions are implemented. MCA graduates can design inclusive feedback systems that value diverse user perspectives and improve product fairness.

48. Discuss the ethical responsibilities of IT professionals in protecting vulnerable groups online.
Answer: Vulnerable groups, such as children or the elderly, face unique online risks like scams and exploitation. IT professionals must design systems with protective measures, such as content filters and reporting mechanisms. MCA graduates should advocate for accessible and secure platforms that prioritize user safety over commercial interests.

49. Analyze how workplace ethics influence client retention in IT service firms.
Answer: Ethical workplaces deliver consistent quality, transparency, and fair pricing, building long-term trust with clients. MCA graduates in service firms should maintain confidentiality, honor commitments, and resolve disputes fairly. Ethical practices strengthen reputations and drive client loyalty in competitive markets.

50. Explain how ethical decision-making helps IT professionals navigate technological disruptions.
Answer: Technological disruptions often present opportunities and challenges, such as replacing jobs with automation. Ethical decision-making guides IT professionals to consider societal impacts, support reskilling initiatives, and design

technologies that benefit all stakeholders. MCA graduates balancing innovation with ethical foresight contribute to sustainable transitions during disruptive changes.

51. Discuss the ethical responsibilities of IT professionals in ensuring cybersecurity for remote workers.
Answer: As remote work becomes widespread, IT professionals have an ethical responsibility to safeguard organizational data and employees' privacy. This includes implementing secure VPNs, enforcing multi-factor authentication, and educating workers on best practices for handling sensitive information. MCA graduates managing such setups should prioritize balancing security measures with user convenience to avoid creating barriers. Ethical practices prevent data breaches and ensure remote employees can work safely without compromising organizational integrity or client trust.

52. Explain how IT professionals can address ethical challenges in developing emotion-detection AI systems.
Answer: Emotion-detection AI systems analyze human expressions or behaviors, raising ethical concerns about privacy, consent, and accuracy. Misinterpretations could lead to biased decisions, especially in areas like recruitment or law enforcement. MCA graduates working on such systems must ensure transparency, obtain informed consent, and design models that are culturally sensitive and fair. Ethical development prevents misuse and fosters public trust in emerging AI technologies.

53. Evaluate the ethical implications of integrating blockchain in voting systems.
Answer: Blockchain offers security and transparency for digital voting but introduces ethical concerns like accessibility, voter anonymity, and potential manipulation by tech-savvy groups. IT professionals must ensure systems are inclusive for all voters, regardless of their technological literacy. MCA graduates should design blockchain voting platforms with strong encryption and robust testing to prevent vulnerabilities. Ethical considerations also include engaging regulators and citizens to build trust in technology-enabled democratic processes.

54. How should IT leaders ethically handle whistleblowing incidents within their organizations?
Answer: When whistleblowing occurs, IT leaders have an ethical duty to investigate impartially, protect the whistleblower from retaliation, and address the reported issue transparently. MCA graduates in leadership roles must promote secure reporting channels and ensure organizational policies support ethical disclosures. Proper handling of whistleblowing fosters a culture of accountability and prevents unethical practices from escalating into crises.

55. Discuss the role of IT professionals in promoting digital inclusion for underprivileged communities.
Answer: Digital inclusion ensures equitable access to technology and the internet for marginalized groups. IT professionals can promote this by developing affordable solutions, supporting infrastructure in remote areas, and creating user-friendly designs for diverse literacy levels. MCA graduates can contribute by volunteering for outreach programs or designing platforms that work on low-spec devices. Ethical commitment to inclusion bridges the digital divide and empowers communities with opportunities for education and economic growth.

56. Analyze how workplace ethics impact decision-making in IT crisis management.
Answer: During IT crises such as data breaches, workplace ethics guide decisions that prioritize transparency, user protection, and legal compliance. Ethical organizations communicate incidents promptly to stakeholders rather than concealing them. MCA graduates in crisis teams should recommend responsible disclosure, focus on mitigation, and avoid blaming individuals unfairly. Ethical crisis management maintains public trust and minimizes long-term reputational damage.

57. Explain how IT professionals should approach ethical dilemmas involving user-generated content platforms.
Answer: Platforms hosting user-generated content face challenges like moderating hate speech, misinformation, or copyright violations. IT professionals must balance freedom of expression with the need to protect users and comply with regulations. MCA graduates can develop transparent moderation policies, employ AI responsibly for detection, and provide appeals processes for users. Ethical management ensures platforms remain safe and trusted spaces for interaction.

58. Discuss the ethical considerations in developing AI-powered autonomous drones.
Answer: Autonomous drones raise ethical issues related to privacy, surveillance, and safety. They can be used for beneficial purposes like disaster relief but also for harmful surveillance or military applications. MCA graduates developing such systems must design safeguards against misuse, incorporate geofencing, and ensure compliance with international laws. Engaging stakeholders and ethical review boards helps align drone technologies with societal values.

59. Evaluate how IT professionals can promote ethical practices in software outsourcing partnerships.
Answer: Outsourcing can create ethical risks like data breaches, unfair labor practices, and lack of accountability. IT professionals should vet outsourcing partners for compliance with ethical standards, ensure contracts specify data security measures, and monitor workflows transparently. MCA graduates working in outsourcing environments should advocate fair wages, cultural sensitivity, and adherence to privacy laws. Ethical outsourcing strengthens trust among clients, vendors, and end-users.

60. Explain how workplace diversity supports ethical innovation in IT companies.
Answer: Diversity in the workplace brings varied perspectives that help identify biases, design inclusive products, and address broader societal needs. Ethical innovation benefits from diverse teams that challenge assumptions and consider underrepresented user groups. MCA graduates should foster inclusive collaborations, ensuring all voices are heard in design and decision-making processes. Such practices result in fairer technologies and enhance an organization's ethical reputation.

61. Discuss how IT professionals can ethically manage AI systems for law enforcement.
Answer: AI systems in law enforcement must be designed ethically to prevent biased profiling and protect civil liberties. MCA graduates working on such projects should ensure transparency, involve oversight committees, and audit algorithms for fairness regularly. Ethical considerations include minimizing false positives, ensuring accountability for decisions, and avoiding mass surveillance practices that violate privacy rights.

62. Analyze the ethical impact of creating persuasive technologies for consumer behavior.
Answer: Persuasive technologies influence consumer behavior, often encouraging purchases or app usage. While they can benefit users (e.g., fitness apps), unethical designs may exploit psychological vulnerabilities for profit. MCA graduates must adopt ethical guidelines like avoiding "dark patterns," providing clear choices, and promoting informed decisions. Ethical persuasion builds user trust and aligns with responsible innovation principles.

63. Explain how IT professionals can balance ethical concerns in facial recognition for public security.
Answer: Facial recognition aids in public security but raises ethical concerns about surveillance, consent, and data misuse. IT professionals must design systems that are transparent, secure, and compliant with privacy laws. MCA graduates should advocate for regulations limiting usage to legitimate purposes, such as locating missing persons, while preventing mass tracking of citizens. Balancing safety with individual rights ensures responsible deployment.

64. Discuss the ethical challenges of using predictive analytics in education systems.
Answer: Predictive analytics in education can help identify at-risk students but also risks labeling or unfairly treating individuals. MCA graduates working in this area should ensure data privacy, avoid reinforcing biases, and involve educators in interpreting predictions. Ethical use of analytics empowers teachers to provide tailored support without compromising student dignity or opportunities.

65. Evaluate how IT professionals should respond when clients demand unethical shortcuts in project delivery.
Answer: Clients may sometimes request shortcuts, like skipping security testing or misreporting progress, to save time or costs. IT professionals have a duty to refuse such practices and explain their risks. MCA graduates should suggest alternative solutions that meet client goals ethically. Upholding standards prevents legal issues and reputational harm for both the professional and the organization.

66. Explain the ethical responsibilities of IT professionals in designing child-friendly digital platforms.
Answer: Designing platforms for children requires heightened attention to privacy, content moderation, and screen-time management. MCA graduates should comply with laws like COPPA, ensure age-appropriate content, and avoid

manipulative engagement tactics. Ethical child-centric design promotes safety and supports healthy digital habits for young users.

67. Discuss how IT professionals can ensure ethical practices in cross-border data transfers.
Answer: Cross-border data transfers involve privacy risks due to differing regulations across countries. IT professionals must ensure compliance with frameworks like GDPR, encrypt data during transit, and seek user consent. MCA graduates managing such transfers should work with legal teams to address jurisdictional challenges ethically and transparently.

68. Analyze the ethical implications of using AI in workplace productivity monitoring tools.
Answer: AI productivity tools can provide valuable insights but also risk invading employee privacy and creating stress. MCA graduates should design systems that focus on supporting workers rather than micromanaging them. Transparency, anonymization, and opt-in options are essential to ensure ethical deployment and maintain employee trust.

69. Explain how IT professionals can address ethical concerns in designing immersive metaverse platforms.
Answer: Metaverse platforms introduce ethical challenges such as user safety, digital addiction, and ownership of virtual assets. MCA graduates should ensure secure environments, promote healthy usage patterns, and protect user data. Ethical considerations also involve designing inclusive spaces where all users feel welcome and respected.

70. Discuss the ethical responsibilities of IT professionals in preventing algorithmic bias in financial services.
Answer: Algorithmic bias in financial services can lead to discriminatory lending or credit scoring practices. IT professionals must ensure training data is representative and audit systems regularly for fairness. MCA graduates working on such projects should prioritize transparency and involve regulators to ensure equitable financial access for all user groups.

71. Evaluate how IT professionals should manage ethical concerns in autonomous delivery robots.
Answer: Autonomous delivery robots raise issues like public safety, job displacement, and data privacy. MCA graduates should ensure these systems are thoroughly tested, compliant with traffic laws, and designed with transparency. Ethical deployment involves engaging communities, minimizing environmental impact, and addressing concerns about replacing human workers.

72. Explain the ethical challenges in designing AI systems for predictive health diagnostics.
Answer: Predictive health diagnostics using AI must avoid inaccuracies that could harm patients or cause undue anxiety. MCA graduates must design systems with clear limitations, involve medical professionals, and ensure patient data security. Ethical AI supports informed decision-making and complements—not replaces—human expertise in healthcare.

73. Discuss how IT professionals can ensure ethical practices in cryptocurrency platforms.
Answer: Cryptocurrency platforms face ethical concerns like fraud, money laundering, and user security. MCA graduates developing such systems should implement strong verification processes, secure wallets, and comply with financial regulations. Ethical practices build trust in the platform and protect users from emerging risks in the crypto market.

74. Analyze the ethical considerations in designing AI systems for emergency response management.
Answer: AI in emergency management can save lives but must be reliable, transparent, and free of biases. MCA graduates should prioritize accuracy, prevent discrimination, and include human oversight for critical decisions. Ethical designs ensure technology aids responders without creating new risks in high-stakes situations.

75. Explain how IT professionals can address ethical concerns in developing brain-computer interface technologies.
Answer: Brain-computer interfaces (BCIs) raise privacy and autonomy issues, as they involve accessing neural data. MCA graduates must ensure informed consent, secure data handling, and avoid exploitative applications. Ethical BCI

development prioritizes user safety and promotes technologies that enhance quality of life without infringing on individual rights.

76. Discuss how IT professionals should address ethical concerns when designing voice assistants.
Answer: Voice assistants collect and process sensitive user data, raising ethical concerns around privacy, consent, and misuse. IT professionals must ensure data is anonymized, securely stored, and only accessed for intended purposes. MCA graduates designing these systems should include clear privacy policies, allow users to delete voice recordings, and avoid eavesdropping functionalities. Ethical design also requires minimizing biases in language recognition to provide equitable experiences across different accents and languages.

77. Explain how IT professionals can promote ethical practices in managing crowdsourced platforms.
Answer: Crowdsourced platforms, like ride-sharing apps or freelance marketplaces, often face ethical challenges including fair pay, data security, and worker rights. IT professionals should implement transparent algorithms for task allocation and fair compensation. MCA graduates must design systems that prevent discrimination and provide secure environments for both workers and users. Ethical management strengthens trust in the platform and creates long-term sustainability.

78. Analyze the ethical challenges of using AI chatbots in customer service for vulnerable populations.
Answer: AI chatbots serving vulnerable groups, such as elderly users or those with disabilities, must be designed with care. Ethical challenges include ensuring accessibility, avoiding misinformation, and escalating critical issues to human agents. MCA graduates should prioritize user safety by incorporating clear disclaimers about chatbot limitations and designing inclusive interfaces. This approach balances automation with empathy, supporting vulnerable users effectively.

79. Discuss the ethical responsibilities of IT professionals in reducing e-waste through sustainable designs.
Answer: E-waste is a growing global concern due to rapid technology upgrades and disposals. IT professionals have an ethical responsibility to design energy-efficient systems, promote repairability, and support recycling initiatives. MCA graduates should advocate for sustainable practices, such as using recyclable materials and developing software that extends hardware lifespan. Ethical action in this area aligns IT development with environmental stewardship.

80. Explain how IT professionals can ensure ethical use of big data analytics in healthcare systems.
Answer: Big data analytics in healthcare provides insights for better treatment but raises ethical concerns about privacy, consent, and potential misuse of sensitive information. MCA graduates should ensure strict compliance with health data protection laws like HIPAA, implement anonymization techniques, and involve medical professionals in data interpretation. Ethical practices maintain patient trust and prevent harm caused by biased or incorrect analyses.

81. Discuss the ethical challenges in designing algorithms for autonomous decision-making systems.
Answer: Autonomous systems, such as self-driving cars or robotic surgeries, make critical decisions that can impact human lives. Ethical challenges include assigning responsibility for failures, mitigating biases, and ensuring transparency in algorithmic logic. MCA graduates must prioritize safety, establish human oversight mechanisms, and adhere to regulatory guidelines to prevent unintended harm and foster public confidence in autonomous technologies.

82. Evaluate how IT professionals should handle ethical dilemmas when working with confidential government projects.
Answer: Confidential government projects involve sensitive data and high societal impact. IT professionals must maintain strict confidentiality, avoid conflicts of interest, and act in the public's best interest. MCA graduates should adhere to ethical standards even when facing pressure to compromise on transparency or privacy. Upholding integrity ensures national security and fosters trust between governments and technology providers.

83. Explain how IT professionals can address ethical concerns in augmented reality (AR) applications.
Answer: AR applications blend virtual and physical environments, raising ethical concerns about user privacy, data security, and psychological effects. MCA graduates designing AR must implement robust privacy settings, prevent misuse of location-based features, and avoid content that could harm vulnerable users. Ethical AR design promotes innovation while safeguarding user rights and ensuring safe interactions in hybrid environments.

84. Discuss the ethical implications of IT professionals implementing surveillance technologies in workplaces.
Answer: Surveillance technologies in workplaces aim to improve security but can infringe on employee privacy and autonomy. MCA graduates developing such systems should recommend transparency in monitoring policies, limit data collection to essential purposes, and provide employees with clear consent options. Ethical practices maintain employee trust and create a balanced approach between organizational security and individual rights.

85. Analyze how IT professionals can ensure fairness in AI-based recruitment systems.
Answer: AI recruitment systems may unintentionally favor certain groups if trained on biased data. IT professionals must use diverse datasets, audit algorithms regularly, and provide transparency in hiring decisions. MCA graduates working on such tools should design them to complement human judgment, ensuring candidates are assessed equitably and reducing systemic discrimination in recruitment processes.

86. Explain how IT professionals should ethically handle user data breaches.
Answer: In the event of a data breach, IT professionals have an ethical obligation to notify affected users promptly, mitigate damages, and prevent future occurrences. MCA graduates should develop incident response plans that prioritize transparency and comply with data protection regulations. Ethical breach management protects user trust and demonstrates accountability in safeguarding sensitive information.

87. Discuss how IT professionals can promote ethical behavior in open-source software collaborations.
Answer: Open-source projects thrive on collaboration but face ethical risks like code theft, lack of attribution, and toxic community behavior. MCA graduates should enforce licensing compliance, credit contributors properly, and foster inclusive communities. Ethical practices encourage innovation and ensure that open-source ecosystems remain healthy and sustainable for all participants.

88. Evaluate the ethical impact of IT professionals designing persuasive technologies for public health campaigns.
Answer: Persuasive technologies in public health, such as fitness apps or vaccination reminders, can encourage positive behaviors but also risk overstepping boundaries if designed manipulatively. MCA graduates should prioritize user autonomy, ensure transparency in persuasive elements, and avoid exploiting vulnerabilities. Ethical designs support user empowerment and build credibility in public health initiatives.

89. Explain the ethical responsibilities of IT professionals in protecting user anonymity on digital platforms.
Answer: Protecting anonymity is critical for users in sensitive contexts like activism or whistleblowing. IT professionals must design platforms with features that secure user identities, such as end-to-end encryption and anonymized data storage. MCA graduates should anticipate threats to anonymity and implement safeguards to prevent unauthorized tracking or breaches. Ethical anonymity protection fosters freedom of expression and user safety.

90. Discuss how IT professionals can ensure ethical practices in developing gamification systems for workplaces.
Answer: Gamification in workplaces can boost engagement but may lead to stress or unhealthy competition if misused. MCA graduates designing such systems should prioritize fairness, transparency, and inclusivity, ensuring that rewards encourage collaboration rather than division. Ethical gamification supports positive motivation while respecting employee autonomy and well-being.

91. Analyze the ethical considerations of IT professionals designing AI-powered predictive policing tools.
Answer: Predictive policing tools raise concerns about bias, privacy, and reinforcing systemic inequalities. MCA graduates must ensure algorithms are fair, transparent, and subject to human oversight. Engaging community stakeholders in design and deployment ensures ethical alignment and prevents misuse that could harm vulnerable populations.

92. Explain how IT professionals can promote ethical practices in the use of biometric authentication.
Answer: Biometric authentication offers convenience but involves sensitive personal data that, if compromised, cannot be changed like passwords. MCA graduates should implement secure storage, minimize data collection, and provide

users with alternatives. Ethical practices ensure user consent and safeguard biometrics from misuse or unauthorized sharing.

93. Discuss how IT professionals can address ethical concerns in the development of social scoring systems.
Answer: Social scoring systems, which evaluate individuals based on behavior, raise concerns about privacy, discrimination, and autonomy. MCA graduates should question the necessity of such systems, advocate for transparency, and prevent them from enabling unfair treatment or surveillance. Ethical resistance to harmful technologies protects fundamental rights and societal fairness.

94. Evaluate how IT professionals should approach ethical challenges in designing smart city infrastructure.
Answer: Smart cities rely on data-driven systems for efficiency but raise ethical challenges like surveillance and data privacy. MCA graduates must design secure, transparent systems with user consent at the core. Involving citizens in decision-making ensures ethical alignment and builds public trust in smart technologies.

95. Explain how IT professionals can ensure ethical behavior in managing artificial intelligence for elder care.
Answer: AI in elder care assists with monitoring and companionship but raises concerns about dignity, privacy, and emotional manipulation. MCA graduates should ensure human oversight, protect sensitive data, and design systems that respect autonomy. Ethical elder care solutions enhance well-being without replacing essential human interaction.

96. Discuss how IT professionals can promote ethical innovation in wearable health devices.
Answer: Wearable health devices collect sensitive data and influence user habits. MCA graduates should prioritize secure data handling, avoid promoting obsessive usage, and ensure inclusivity for diverse populations. Ethical innovation in wearables empowers users to manage health responsibly while protecting privacy and autonomy.

97. Analyze how IT professionals should ethically handle algorithmic transparency in financial decision-making tools.
Answer: Financial tools driven by algorithms must be transparent to avoid misleading users. MCA graduates should design explainable models, provide clear disclaimers about limitations, and allow human intervention. Ethical transparency ensures fairness and prevents discriminatory practices in sensitive financial contexts.

98. Explain the ethical responsibilities of IT professionals in regulating content moderation algorithms.
Answer: Content moderation algorithms must balance free expression with the removal of harmful material. MCA graduates should design fair, unbiased systems and provide appeal mechanisms for users. Ethical content moderation ensures platforms remain safe without unjustly silencing voices.

99. Discuss how IT professionals can promote sustainable practices in data center operations.
Answer: Data centers consume significant energy, impacting the environment. MCA graduates should advocate for renewable energy sources, optimize server efficiency, and promote virtualization to reduce physical hardware needs. Ethical sustainability efforts align IT operations with global environmental goals.

100. Evaluate how IT professionals can ensure ethical use of AI in mental health diagnosis tools.
Answer: AI tools for mental health diagnosis must avoid overreliance, ensure accuracy, and protect patient privacy. MCA graduates should involve healthcare professionals in development and provide clear disclaimers to users. Ethical AI supports mental health care as a supplement, not a replacement, for qualified human expertise.

101. Explain how IT professionals can ensure ethical practices when designing AI for autonomous vehicles.
Answer: AI for autonomous vehicles involves life-critical decisions, making ethics paramount. MCA graduates must ensure algorithms prioritize safety, avoid discrimination in decision-making (e.g., favoring pedestrians over passengers), and include mechanisms for human intervention in emergencies. Transparent communication about system limitations, rigorous testing, and compliance with legal standards are vital. Ethical practices build public trust and ensure the technology serves society without compromising safety or fairness.

102. Discuss the ethical responsibilities of IT professionals in regulating online hate speech.
Answer: IT professionals managing platforms with user-generated content face challenges in balancing free speech

with protection from harm. MCA graduates should design moderation algorithms that detect and remove hate speech while respecting diverse viewpoints. Transparency, appeal mechanisms, and collaboration with stakeholders help avoid biases in regulation. Ethical moderation ensures safe digital spaces while safeguarding rights to expression.

103. Analyze how IT professionals can ethically manage surveillance in smart home devices.
Answer: Smart home devices gather extensive personal data, raising ethical concerns about surveillance and misuse. MCA graduates must prioritize privacy by incorporating strong encryption, anonymization techniques, and clear user consent protocols. Users should have control over data collection and sharing. Ethical management fosters trust in smart home ecosystems while protecting individuals from potential exploitation or unauthorized access.

104. Explain the ethical challenges of deploying AI-based lie detection systems in law enforcement.
Answer: AI lie detection systems risk inaccuracies, biases, and violations of privacy. MCA graduates developing such tools must ensure high accuracy rates, involve oversight from legal experts, and establish transparency in their use. Ethical deployment requires clear guidelines to prevent misuse and protect individuals' rights, ensuring justice is not compromised by overreliance on technology.

105. Discuss how IT professionals can ensure ethical practices in cryptocurrency mining operations.
Answer: Cryptocurrency mining consumes enormous energy, contributing to environmental harm. MCA graduates should explore sustainable alternatives, such as proof-of-stake mechanisms, and advocate for renewable energy use in mining setups. Ethical practices also involve educating stakeholders about environmental impacts and supporting regulations that promote eco-friendly blockchain technologies.

106. Evaluate the ethical implications of using AI for emotion recognition in workplace performance evaluations.
Answer: Emotion recognition AI in workplaces can lead to privacy violations and biased assessments. MCA graduates must ensure that such tools are used only with informed consent, provide transparent insights into decision-making, and avoid overreliance on AI for human emotions. Ethical implementation supports fair evaluations and preserves employee dignity.

107. Explain how IT professionals can promote ethical innovation in virtual healthcare systems.
Answer: Virtual healthcare systems require secure, inclusive, and transparent designs. MCA graduates must ensure patient confidentiality, comply with medical data laws, and avoid reinforcing health inequities. Ethical innovation in telemedicine enables access for underserved populations while maintaining high standards of care and trust.

108. Discuss the ethical considerations in designing persuasive educational technologies.
Answer: Persuasive educational tools should motivate learners without manipulation or addiction risks. MCA graduates must design systems that respect user autonomy, offer clear objectives, and avoid exploitative gamification. Ethical educational technologies foster long-term learning habits and enhance student engagement responsibly.

109. Analyze how IT professionals can address ethical challenges in designing AI-powered hiring chatbots.
Answer: AI hiring chatbots may unintentionally filter candidates based on biased algorithms. MCA graduates must implement diverse training datasets, ensure transparency in decision-making, and provide options for human oversight. Ethical design minimizes discrimination and supports equitable hiring processes across organizations.

110. Explain the ethical responsibilities of IT professionals in managing user consent in IoT ecosystems.
Answer: IoT devices often operate silently in the background, collecting continuous data. MCA graduates must ensure explicit user consent, provide clear data usage policies, and allow users to control what information is shared. Ethical consent management builds user trust and prevents violations of privacy.

111. Discuss how IT professionals can ensure ethical practices in gamification for healthcare.
Answer: Gamification in healthcare motivates healthy behaviors but must avoid overuse or dependency. MCA graduates should design systems that encourage balance, ensure data privacy, and comply with medical guidelines. Ethical gamification supports user well-being and aligns technology with public health goals.

112. Evaluate the ethical implications of using predictive analytics in employee retention strategies.
Answer: Predictive analytics for retention may inadvertently label employees unfairly or breach privacy. MCA graduates must ensure data is anonymized, insights are used constructively, and employees are informed of monitoring practices. Ethical use of analytics fosters trust and avoids undermining morale.

113. Explain how IT professionals can ethically design blockchain-based voting systems.
Answer: Blockchain voting offers transparency but raises accessibility and privacy concerns. MCA graduates should design systems that allow verifiability without compromising voter anonymity and ensure usability for all demographics. Ethical blockchain systems strengthen democratic processes while preventing misuse or exclusion.

114. Discuss the ethical responsibilities of IT professionals in designing AI tools for content creation.
Answer: AI content creation tools risk plagiarism, misinformation, and job displacement. MCA graduates must prioritize transparency, include watermarks for AI-generated content, and design tools that assist rather than replace human creativity. Ethical development balances innovation with societal responsibility.

115. Analyze how IT professionals can address ethical concerns in wearable fitness trackers.
Answer: Fitness trackers collect sensitive health and location data, raising privacy concerns. MCA graduates should ensure data is encrypted, provide clear usage policies, and allow users to control sharing settings. Ethical designs empower users without compromising their privacy or autonomy.

116. Explain how IT professionals can promote digital well-being through ethical design principles.
Answer: Digital well-being involves reducing technology's negative effects on mental health. MCA graduates can design apps with features like time limits, focus modes, and reminders for offline breaks. Ethical design respects user autonomy and promotes healthy tech usage patterns.

117. Discuss the ethical challenges of AI in automating hiring decisions for gig economy workers.
Answer: Automating gig worker hiring may result in unfair evaluations or exclusion of certain demographics. MCA graduates must design algorithms that are unbiased, transparent, and provide recourse for appeals. Ethical AI supports fair access to gig opportunities and reduces systemic inequalities.

118. Evaluate the ethical implications of designing smart wearables for children.
Answer: Wearables for children involve risks like tracking misuse and privacy breaches. MCA graduates must ensure strict parental controls, comply with child data protection laws, and avoid features that promote excessive screen time. Ethical designs safeguard children's safety and development.

119. Explain how IT professionals can address ethical concerns in virtual reality therapy tools.
Answer: VR therapy offers innovative treatment options but raises issues around safety, privacy, and efficacy. MCA graduates should ensure clear user guidelines, involve medical professionals in design, and avoid manipulative immersive experiences. Ethical VR therapy prioritizes patient well-being and complements traditional treatment approaches.

120. Discuss how IT professionals can ensure ethical practices in AI systems for disaster management.
Answer: AI for disaster management must prioritize accuracy and fairness to avoid resource misallocation. MCA graduates should design systems that involve human oversight, protect sensitive community data, and ensure inclusivity in aid distribution. Ethical AI enhances response effectiveness without causing unintended harm.

9 789369 723126

Printed at Repro India Ltd.